I AM WITH YOU

The Archbishop of Canterbury's Lent Book 2016

KATHRYN GREENE-McCREIGHT

B L O O M S B U R Y

LONDON · OXFORD · NEW YORK · NEW DELHI · SYDNEY

Bloomsbury Continuum
An imprint of Bloomsbury Publishing Plc

50 Bedford Square
London
WC1B 3DP
UK

1385 Broadway
New York
NY 10018
USA

www.bloomsbury.com

Bloomsbury, Continuum and the Diana logo are trademarks of Bloomsbury
Publishing Plc

First published 2015

© Kathryn Greene-McCreight, 2015

Kathryn Greene-McCreight has asserted her right under the Copyright,
Designs and Patents Act, 1988, to be identified as Author of this work.

British Library Cataloguing-in-Publication Data
A catalogue record for this book is available from the British Library.

Library of Congress Cataloguing-in-Publication data has been applied for.

ISBN: PB: 9781472915238
ePDF: 9781472915245
ePub: 9781472915252

2 4 6 8 10 9 7 5 3 1

Printed and bound in Great Britain by CPI Group (UK) Ltd, Croydon CR0 4YY

To find out more about our authors and books visit
www.bloomsbury.com. Here you will find extracts, author interviews,
details of forthcoming events and the option to sign up for our newsletters.

CONTENTS

FOREWORD BY THE ARCHBISHOP OF CANTERBURY

I first came across Kathryn Greene-McCreight when I read her book, *Darkness is My Only Companion*. It is a personal account of her struggle with depression and a theological reflection on the nature of mental illness. For me, it was one of those rare books that reshapes the understanding. Its utter transparency and integrity moved me deeply, while its sophistication and profundity sparked some fruitful thinking.

So when a few days later I was wondering who might write the Lent book for 2016, Kathryn's name jumped readily to mind. Others involved in the process felt equally positive about the choice, and the book entirely fulfils my hopes in asking Kathryn to write it.

It's a very different kind of book; Kathryn is no 'one-trick pony'. This is a meditation for Lent on God's presence, light and darkness, all set in the context of the Offices of the Benedictine day.

It is a book that operates on a number of levels. Each chapter can stand alone. For devotional use in Lent, I'd recommend that the chapters are taken a week at a time.

It is beautifully written: the thoughts unfold gently before the eyes as one reads. They lead us inexorably back to the heart of orthodox Christianity: which is not a set of dogmatic or doctrinal propositions, nor a way of life, let alone a set of rules – although there are aspects that spring out of the richness of the Christian life in each of these areas. It is about the lived experience of the presence of God in all circumstances and all times, including everything that life can throw at us.

As such, this book is about growing closer to God. That is at the heart of a good Lent. We come to a time of fasting, discipline and study, in order that we may renew our knowledge of His presence. That involves a stripping of those things that divide us from God, developing our obedience to His call and venturing deeper into the fire of His love.

The themes of light and darkness, and the use of the pattern of the Offices, give contrast and stability to the unfolding chapters. Through the book we travel through day and night, the reality of human experience lived through our lives. At the end the dawn brightens with the hope and certainty of resurrection, the knowledge that in the grace and love of God we are called to eternal life with the one who smashes down the barriers of death.

As well as contrast and the stability of the Offices, there is the interaction with God. How does He come to us and speak to us? Sometimes it is through messengers and angels; sometimes it is through His revealed presence; sometimes it is through the changes and chances of life in all its challenge and complexity.

Someone once described to me two preachers: one who sounded sophisticated, yet the more you thought about it the less there was; and the other who sounded simple, yet the more you thought about it the more there was. Kathryn is in the latter category. This is a book to be picked up and put down quietly, not read at a sitting or in a rush. Where something is too demanding, I recommend that you move on and come back to it. The book gives one permission to say, 'I'm not quite there yet'.

As with the rhythm of Benedictine life in the monastery, the Offices repeat themselves day by day. After a week, one may feel to have seen virtually all there is. That is the point at which the growing really begins: the process of deepening is through repetition.

I trust that as you read and reflect on this book you will find that deepening. It will bring you to the glorious dawn of Easter, filled with confidence and joy.

+Justin Cantuar

Lambeth Palace

Feast of the Transfiguration, 2015

INTRODUCTION:
I AM WITH YOU

Lent is traditionally a time of self-examination and repentance as we prepare for Easter and the resurrection of Jesus. If we think of Easter as light, we might think of Lent as preparing our eyes to behold that light. Light helps us see where we are headed, but sometimes it can hurt our eyes.[1]

Imagine going from a completely darkened room immediately into bright daylight. We might shield our eyes as we become accustomed to the light. Gradually exposing ourselves to light keeps us from squinting in pain. Here is God's mercy: the sun rises slowly. It could have been different, I suppose, but the disciples find the tomb empty in the morning. The darkness is slowly conquered as the rising sun leads in the morning. Only then do the disciples behold the Light of the World. It is for this Easter light that we prepare the eyes of our souls during Lent. We move from morning through the daytime, past the night, beyond the dawn to the morning of the resurrection.

In order to recognize the presence of God in light, as did the disciples on that first Easter, we might try first to learn about the identity of the Risen One. How do we do this? We turn to Scripture. There we are guided in discerning the identity of the

One who greets us in the resurrection light of the New Creation. As Paul says, on the last day the trumpet will sound and the dead will be raised, and we shall all be changed (1 Cor. 15.52). Easter is a foretaste of that last day, of that trumpet call, of that New Creation.

But first, a word on what it might mean for us to make such a bold claim – that God could be present.

Bidden or Unbidden, God is Present

Carl Jung (1875–1961), the father of analytic psychology, would probably approve of our title, *I Am With You*. Among other things, he thought that we humans are fundamentally religious beings. Exactly what Jung understood by the word 'religious' is not clear to me. I do have a clearer sense, though, of what religion, for him, was *not*.

Apparently, during his graduate studies, Jung was rummaging through collections of Latin proverbs. A saying by the Humanist scholar Erasmus of Rotterdam (1466–1536) struck him in particular: *Vocatus atque non vocatus, Deus aderit*. We might translate this into English as 'Bidden or unbidden, God is present,' or maybe more loosely as 'Whether you like it or not, God is here.' Jung affixed this quotation over the door of his home in Zurich, and it is said that these were his last words. The proverb is also carved on his tombstone.

Ironically, these words seem to have come from a yet earlier source. What is far more interesting, though, is that the proverb is often translated by Jung's followers as 'Bidden or unbidden, *the god* is present.' While this may indeed have been Jung's understanding of Erasmus, I seriously doubt that Erasmus himself would have approved of such a translation. For Erasmus '*Vocatus atque non vocatus, Deus aderit*' would not have referred to a generic deity ('the god') but to *the* God of Abraham, Isaac and Jacob, the God of Jesus Christ.

Jung was a man of his age, just as Erasmus was a man of his. And our own age, in turn, inherits in many ways, more from Jung than from Erasmus. Like Jung, we often choke on the scandal of particularity. We, too, tend to prefer universal ideas rather than specifics. With regard to Jesus, this preference is expressed in Judas' mocking song in the 1970s' rock opera *Jesus Christ Superstar* by Andrew Lloyd Webber: 'If you'd come today you would have reached a whole nation; Israel in 4 BC had no mass communication.' Specificity is so limiting. For us modern folk, the idea that God is 'in the details' is more of a problem than we may think.

Our culture tends to see religion as did Jung: a generalized spirituality that may offer an experience of a divine presence, a non-specific god. Such an experience would certainly be tame compared to an encounter with the God of Israel, the God of Jesus Christ. But it is specifically the God of Jesus Christ who is the One whose identity we come to discern through Scripture and the worship of the Church. The identity of this God is not generic. 'This is my body, this is my blood ...'

The seventeenth-century philosopher Blaise Pascal put the matter of God's specificity this way: 'The God of Abraham, Isaac and Jacob, not the god of the philosophers.' Here we see what Jung and many of us prefer to avoid: the God of the Bible is to be found in a specific relationship within a narrated history. That God is the One who is with us, who is present, whether we like it or not.

This book has become, with my slowly dawning awareness, a very brief biblical theology of God's presence as light in darkness. It is a simple sketch of God's identity as we find it in Scripture. Only when we learn who God is in Scripture can we begin to grasp what it might mean for God to be with us. This is partly what Pascal was getting at: we encounter God's presence through a shared history told in the Scriptures and in the worship of the Church. If there is a God who can truly be present, it would not be a god defined by a set of concepts or a construct of ideas. Presence only comes through relationship and encounter.

The Caravaggio painting on the cover of this book is 'The Inspiration of St Matthew' ('*San Matteo e l'angelo*'). Matthew writes at his desk in the lower-left quadrant while the angel hovers above him to the right. Ethereal swathes of white cloth swirl around the angel, drawing our attention to the upper right of the painting. All is dark there, except for the angel, who cuts through the darkness, casting light on the Evangelist's face and his book. The angel counts on his fingers, as though instructing St Matthew what to write, mediating God's message to the Evangelist. One wonders: is the angel helping him remember the list of names of Jesus' ancestors?

A genealogy opens Matthew's own account of God's presence in Jesus. Caravaggio's angel helps the Evangelist to sketch the identity of the Messiah born of the house of David (Mt. 1). Matthew is depicted as a simple man. While he is educated enough to be able to write, he depends on the angel's instruction. Matthew seems to have hurried to his table: his clothes are in disarray and his feet are still dirty from the road. It seems that in his haste Matthew has knocked his stool off balance: it tips toward us, as though about to tumble out of the frame.

This painting introduces some of the themes of *I Am With You*: the contrast of light and dark; the mediating presence of God in the angel; the identity of Jesus as tied to the house of David; the key role of Scripture in introducing Jesus to us; the everyday-ness of our encounter with Christ in the trappings of our own earthly life; and the Jesus who at the end of the Gospel according to Matthew promises his own presence with us.

I have arranged the chapters of this book to evoke the monastic hours of prayer. These hours are based on, but expanded from, the biblical tradition of seven times of daily worship:

> Seven times a day I praise you
>
> for your righteous ordinances. (Ps. 119.164)

By the ninth century in the Western Christian tradition there had developed eight 'hours' or times set aside for prayer in the monasteries: lauds, prime, terce, sext, none, vespers and compline, and the night office. Because these words are not familiar to most of us any more, I present the hours differently, simply as times of the day: morning, noon, afternoon, evening and night, which has been divided into the three traditional Hebrew watches (cf. Lam. 2.19; Judg. 7.19; Exod. 14.24).

However, I choose not to end the 'hours' with night. In all due respect to the monastic tradition, its sequence mis-represents Scripture. Evening in Scripture does not close the day, but begins it: 'And there was evening and there was morning, the first day' (Gen. 1.5). Unlike our Jewish brothers and sisters, we Gentile Christians pay little attention to this verse, although it is profoundly important for how we understand God's presence, especially when we find that all is dark. This verse assures us that ultimately we are not left in the darkness of night. Darkness is not the final word. Darkness is enclosed by light, not the other way around. Morning comes after the night. Light marks the end of the night. Morning is not just the beginning of what follows but more properly is the end of what came before: the night. We encounter the risen Jesus in the morning, in the New Creation. Time itself is transformed in the resurrection.

At the close of the Gospel according to Matthew, we read that Jesus commissions the disciples to baptize and to teach. He then promises them his presence: 'And remember, I am with you always, to the end of the age' (Mt. 28.20). We hear that word addressed also to us in our turn.

The word that closes the entire Bible is itself a promise: 'Surely, I am coming soon' (Rev. 22.20). It is a promise of presence that elicits our response in fervent prayer: 'Amen, come, Lord Jesus.' The writer of Revelation follows this with a blessing on those who pray: 'The grace of the Lord Jesus be with all the saints' (22.21). God's presence comes in the promise of God's gift of Himself, and it is a blessing.

Nothing escapes the Lord's notice. Indeed, even our hidden secrets are present to Him. So let us act in everything we do as if He were dwelling within us, so that we may be His temples and He may be our God within us.

IGNATIUS, LETTER TO THE EPHESIANS, 15.3

New Haven, Connecticut

Holy Week, 2015

1

Morning: God's Presence in the Beginning

In the beginning when God created the heavens and the earth,
the earth was a formless void and darkness covered the face
of the deep, while a wind from God swept over the face of the
waters. Then God said, 'Let there be light'; and there was light.
And God saw that the light was good; and God separated
the light from the darkness. God called the light Day, and the
darkness he called Night. And there was evening and there was
morning, the first day.

GENESIS 1.1–5

The claim that the God of Scripture speaks is more preposterous than we might think, because it means that God is not simply the object of our contemplation, or even of our worship. The claim that God speaks means that God is not a concept, not an idol. These do not speak.

One form of speech is address. Address creates a relationship, an intimacy that extends beyond that established by mere speech. The power to address is what makes the God of Israel different from many other deities of the Ancient Near East, and from most of the gods of our own making as well.

The God of the Bible encounters us in a relationship created by address. And God's address requires a response. The God of the Bible acts, covenants, promises, rescues, loves. God's presence first comes to us in speech at creation when God calls light into being.

God's Presence in Speech at Creation: Light

The God who will address us as light at Easter is the God who spoke light into being at the beginning of the Bible. In Genesis 1, creating light is God's first act. The Gospel according to John begins by telling us that God Himself is light, which neither admits nor allows darkness (1.5). God is the source of light; God is the shining of the light; God is the illuminating that the light accomplishes. God is that light itself.

Without light, of course, there would be no darkness. Darkness descends only as light wanes. Darkness is the shadow that light casts behind whatever obstructs its path. Nothing is hidden in light. All is exposed.

but everything exposed by the light becomes visible, for everything that becomes visible is light. Therefore it says, 'Sleeper, awake! Rise from the dead, and Christ will shine on you.' (Eph. 5.13–14)

The one who sees in secret dwells in eternal light, and exposes our works. Light distinguishes good from evil. Light disperses darkness, and even the love of darkness.

When I was a little girl, we lived in a wooded area with much wildlife. One day, we found that somehow a possum had wandered into a back passage in our garage. We knew that, if it did not return to its natural habitat, it would die, so we tried to coax it out into the open area of the garage where it could escape and be free to return to its home. But we were trying to do so with the aid of a flashlight. Possums are night creatures. Their eyes cannot bear the light. While we thought we were helping the poor creature, we were only making it more frightened. It froze stiff and wouldn't move. Finally, we left it alone, and without the light shining in its eyes, it was able in the darkness to flee to its home.

God's light, like our flashlight trained on that possum, exposes all who prefer darkness. God's light repels night creatures who cannot bear the pain of being exposed, who fear the light and who want to remain hidden in the dark. Light draws those who want to be illumined, who want to dwell in the light of truth (Jn 1.9).

Without light, we cannot see. Without light, there can be no life. It is light that marks days, seasons and years. It does this by the help of the 'lesser lights' made on the fourth day: sun, moon and stars. To say that God is light is to say also that God is life. Jesus is that light and that life: 'In Him was life, and the life was the light of all' (Jn 1.4).

The Creation: Genesis 1–3

While the Creation story in Genesis has parallels in the literature of the Ancient Near East, the story in the Bible is quite distinct. The similarities are very interesting, but it is the differences that are the gems to mine in interpretation.

Unlike many of the creation stories of the Ancient Near East, the creation account in Genesis is completely uninterested in the question of God's origins. God's existence prior to and outside of His creation is simply a given. The text does not attempt to assert, prove or explain the Creator's existence.

Again, in the Creation story of Genesis, there is no definition of God. There is no doctrine of God. There is no philosophical speculation about God's nature, either in God's acts or through His address to humanity.

This means that for the authors and editors of Genesis, the words of the Reformation refrain many millenia later apply: God is known through God alone. The way we come to know God is first through God. God is not introduced as though needing some sort of letter of recommendation. God's presence is how God introduces Himself. That introduction comes first through speech, and then through address. God's speech and address take many forms throughout the Bible, but all of them point to God's presence: I Am With You.

God's Address

On the first day of creation, God's speech is directed into thin silence and emptiness. There, God calls all light into being through His spoken word: '"Let there be light"; and there was light' (Gen. 1.3). God's spoken word at the creation of light is not yet properly God's address, because as of yet in the story there is no creature to receive God's speech. This is a mystery to behold: the God of Israel is both completely independent of creation, and yet thoroughly delighted in and even fascinated by it. This free God is bound to creation in a relationship of care, nurture and grace.

God's presence as light comes to us in the very first scene of Scripture, and we find it in the form of speech. These first days of creation are called into being by God's speech: 'Let there be ...' (Gen. 1.3, 6, 14, 15); 'Let the waters ... and the dry land be ...' (1.9); 'Let the earth ...' (1.11); 'Let the waters ...' (1.20); 'Let the earth ...' (1.24). The forms of these verbs are impersonal commands (or 'jussives'). This is all speech, but is not yet properly address. Right now, it is simply an impersonal 'Let there be ...'

On the first five days of creation, God creates light, earth, skies, vegetation and some of the living creatures. God's actual address to creation itself does not come until the fifth day. There we find it in the form of a blessing yoked with a command directed to the sea creatures and the winged creatures He had already made with the divine fiat: 'Let the waters bring forth ...' (Gen. 1.20).

This blessing is given in address to the creatures of the fifth day in a form of a command: 'Be fruitful and multiply and fill the waters and the seas and let birds multiply on the earth' (Gen. 1.22). The very nature of the command emphasizes that God's will for creation is life: the continuation of God's own work in creation.

But on the sixth day we find two types of creation God enacts via different types of speech, address, and even different verbs of creating. God's address in the context of the creation of *adam* first comes as self-address. It seems that the other creatures do not 'count' as proper conversation partners for God, but *adam* will. God's self-address here, distinct from all previous acts of creation, indicates a special relationship with *adam*: 'Let us make *adam* ...' (Gen. 1.26). Instead of the earlier 'Let there be ...' we read 'Let us make ...'

On the first half of the sixth day, God creates the land animals. The narrator uses the common Hebrew verb (*'asah*) which we translate into English 'to make'. On the second half of the sixth day, God's action takes the Hebrew verb (*bara'*) which we translate into English 'to create'. While the verb *bara'* has occurred twice previously in the chapter (1.1 and 1.21), it is used on the sixth day with regard only to God's creation of *adam*, the human creature.

On the sixth day, in God's self-address ('Let us make...'; Gen. 1.26), it is as though we are overhearing a conversation within the Divine Council. The generic Hebrew noun for 'God', *Elohim*, itself evokes a plural form. In much of the history of Christian biblical interpretation, this 'Royal We' speech is heard as an inner conversation among the persons of the Holy Trinity: Father, Son and Holy Spirit.

The Image of God: Relationship

Trying to think about the riddle of what it means for *adam* to be made in the image and likeness of God demands that we read the text closely; this means, as we have seen, to take seriously God's address. Address as speech requires an addressee, someone else, and thus creates a relationship. Address creates a 'Thou' for the 'I' of the speaker. Rather than the impersonal command forms we have been hearing until now ('Let there be ...'), God's speech as address creates a relationship with the human creature. There is no other way into that relationship apart from God's gracious and free address.

Two distinctions are introduced at 1.26. In addition to God's first self-address or internal conversation of the 'Royal We', we find that God becomes for the first time in the narrative the subject of an active verb. God commands and claims *adam* as the object of His address, drawing the human one from his very moment of creation into the orbit of relationship with the Creator.

The phrase in Gen. 1.26–27, 'in the image and likeness of God', has been a topic of much discussion throughout the centuries among biblical interpreters, Jewish and Christian alike. What is this image? Is it power? Is it rationality? Is it freedom of choice? As I read the text, it is none of these.

So God created *adam* in His image, in the image of God He created him [or it], male and female He created them.

One of the most important things to note at this point in the text is that there is no 'humanity' to speak of at all yet, if by 'humanity' we mean a collection of humans. This is not the suggestion of the text. *Adam*, this human creature, is singular until the mention that *adam* is made in the image of God as male and female. Only at that point does *adam* take a plural pronoun and becomes a 'them'. This itself seems to be what it is to be created in God's image: to be in relation, not only with God, but with each other. Our relation to one another here is only defined in terms of sexual differentiation. At this point in the narrative, there are no other distinctions to be made within 'humanity': not race, not creed, not ethnicity. The only distinction noted within our species is between male and female.

Adam as a single noun (not a name at this point in the text) might be better translated 'human one' rather than 'humanity', but because in English 'human one' is awkward, I will leave it untranslated here. I will simply render the Hebrew letters in their English equivalents, that is, transliterated. This way of transliterating the human creature as *adam* will become important later in Genesis. In Genesis 2, *adam* is made from the *adamah*, the mud, the dirt, the ground. The human creature *adam* thus bears a strong relationship to the dirt or mud from which it and we in our turn come, and to which we will return. 'Remember you are dust, and to dust you shall return.' We might therefore also translate *adam* as 'muddy one'.

But in Genesis 1.27 there is no generic 'humanity' in any meaningful sense until the words 'male and female' appear (Hebrew: *zakar unqevah* [Gen. 1.27]). Our true humanity is in our having been made in the image of God, male and female (1.26; cf. 3.22). And it is only at this point (Gen. 1.28) that God actually addresses *adam*, who is now a plurality: *adam*-as-male-and-female. Until this point, God's words are only speech, as though He is talking to Himself. But as we saw earlier, with the creatures of the fifth day, God's address to *adam*-as-male-and-female comes in the form of a blessing as command: 'And God blessed them and said *to them*, "Be fruitful and multiply …"' (Gen. 1.28).

Adam-as-male-and-female is blessed in the form of the command that is structured similarly to the command given to the creatures of the fifth day. But God's first address to *adam* is different from that to the creatures of the fifth day. God has just created *adam* in His image and likeness: male and female. The blessing in the form of the command (to be fruitful and multiply) here has a different spin: it creates a life-giving relationship between the human creatures, male and female.

God's blessing on *adam*-as-male-and-female includes the bestowal of gifts: 'See I have given [to] you [plural] every plant yielding seed …' (Gen. 1.29). *Adam*-as-male-and-female is set in relationship to other living creatures; *adam*-as-male-and-female becomes the first indirect object in the narrative. The command to guard creation is detailed here. While *adam*-as-male-and-female is the apex of the created order of the first six days, *adam*-as-male-and-female is clearly not the only creature of significance. *Adam*-as-male-and-female is the first among many (or the seventh among many, created on the second half of the sixth day), but *adam*-as-male-and-female shares the blessing of being with and for the other creatures.

We too are recipients of gifts freely given and unearned. As such, we too are agents in our own right, capable of making moral choices. We too are under command ('Be fruitful …'), and as such we are given a purpose.

This means, also, that like the Creator we have freedom. But our freedom, unlike that of the Creator, is constrained. Our freedom comes in only two forms: either to obey or to disobey God's command. Otherwise, God's address would not be stated in command form. Rather, it might be more like the earlier impersonal commands: 'Let there be …'.

Receiving a command is different from hearing a suggestion. A command can only be either obeyed or disobeyed, while a suggestion can be heeded, ignored, or anything in between. A command sets up a relationship of responsibility, but a suggestion carries no such hint of commitment. To be commanded means, in fact, to be given a degree of freedom: to obey or disobey.

God's blessing-as-command is like a marriage proposal. A response is required: either a yes or a no. And it must be a lived response, not merely a verbal response, nor a cognitive response. It involves our very being. If our response to our divine Lover's proposal is to be yes, our lives are completely turned around, and we enter a new relationship. We hear such a response in the praises of the Church:

> You are worthy, our Lord and God,
>
> to receive glory and honour and power,
>
> for you created all things,
>
> and by your will they existed and were created. (Rev. 4.11)

Rejecting God's proposal is also life-changing. It creates a breach between the One who proposes and the one who rejects. We will find such a turn in the plot in Genesis 3. But for now, *adam*-as-male-and-female is addressed, blessed and commanded in a relationship of gift and demand. And God's first true address to us is a blessing about the goodness of human life. It is a command toward our future amidst this amazingly good creation.

The four-fold structure of God's communication shows us the following. First, God's self-address casts *adam* as a direct object: 'Let us make *adam* ...' (Gen. 1.26). God is the subject and agent. *Adam* is the object.

Second, God addresses them in blessing ('they' have become at this point a 'them'), which sets them in relation to Him: 'God blessed them ...' (1.28a). This blessing comes in the form of a command in the second-person plural. This blessing/command then sets them in relation to each other: 'Be fruitful and multiply...' (1.28b).

Third, God commands them again in the second-person plural, but here they are to be subjects in their own right in relation to all of creation: 'Fill the earth and subdue it ...' (1.28c).

Fourth, God's address in the second-person plural casts them as indirect objects in relationship to all creation: 'See, I have given [to] you ...' (1.29). They are to 'subdue' creation (1.28c), so they must in some respect be 'above' it. Yet they are the recipients of creation and in need of it, so they must in some respect be 'under' it (1.29). In fact, they need the rest of creation more than the rest of creation needs them. They need creation for their very sustenance and survival (1.29, 'for food'), but creation only needs the stewardship of *adam*-as-male-and-female. This steward is the responsible one, and also the servant. The animals do not have this role, this special blessing.

Relationship: Humans and Animals

The theme of interdependence of humans and animals runs throughout the Bible, from Abraham's flocks to the animals in the Gospel nativity scenes. The book of Jonah ends on this note:

> And should I not be concerned about Nineveh, that great city, in which there are more than a hundred and twenty thousand persons who do not know their right hand from their left, and also many animals? (Jon. 4.11)

The most popular example of this interdependence between humans and animals is the Flood story in Genesis 6–9. Noah is commanded to gather not only his family but also every variety of animal into the ark to save them from the waters of death. This follows the earlier detail in Genesis 1 of the priority of animals over vegetation. Noah does not argue with God about the impending destruction of the earth (as will Abraham over the destruction of Sodom in Gen. 19). But building the ark is not Noah's own intuition, his own undertaking, his own plan. It is simply God's command. Humans and animals belong together, not only for the benefit of humans, but also for the well-being of the animals. We exist in a relation of being-for and being-with each other.

Here is sheer grace: God commands Noah to bring into the ark even the unclean animals. We will find the distinction between clean and unclean animals only later in the story of the people of Israel. These categories will become important for Israel only in its relationship with its covenant God. The grace of God embraces even the class of animals that will become to some extent 'unnecessary' to Israel, except in so far as they will become one of the means for testing and proving Israel's faithfulness to the God who chooses in freedom. With the inclusion here of the unclean animals, there is a sense in which we find a foreshadowing of the Gospel's inclusion of the Gentiles. Like unclean animals, Gentiles as such will be of no benefit to the chosen people. They are included only by way of blessing, despite their not-chosen-ness.

All elements of creation dwelling in relationship find themselves in a position of vulnerability one to the other. And vulnerability is one of the key markers of creaturely existence, and, above all, human existence. This pulls the rug out from under our contemporary understanding of human 'individuality' and indeed 'autonomy'. As Eastern Orthodox theologian John Zizioulas remarks:

> being a person is fundamentally different from being an individual or a 'personality', for a person cannot be imagined in himself but only within his relationships.[2]

To say that human creatures, indeed all instances of the created order, are fundamentally constituted for relationship may sound obvious. And yet, if we really think about it, such a view can come across as offensive to the ears of our broader culture. In the West especially, we value so highly the rights of the individual that true interdependence is hard for us even to imagine, much less to bear or defend. But, according to the Genesis creation story, there is no human individuality apart from relationship. There is no true humanity without other creatures of God.

Animals and humans, both created on the sixth day, will share an intertwined destiny for good and for ill throughout the rest of the Bible. This vocation of interdependence will continue right up to the manger scene at Bethlehem, where Jesus is born among ox and ass and sheep and goats. This vocation of interdependence will continue beyond the crucifixion of the Lamb of God, who is paradoxically the Good Shepherd who lays down his life for his sheep. It will continue through the Passover of the Upper Room, past the Empty Tomb and into the eighth day, when creation in its entirety will be healed and made afresh.

Adam and God's Presence in Creation

Adam is made 'in the image of God'. This detail gives us the sense that *adam* is a token and sign of God's presence in the world. *Adam* sums up and represents God in creation. In this, *adam* steps in as the type of the One to Come, Jesus (Rom. 5.14).[3] Jesus himself is the 'last Adam' (1 Cor. 15.45). Creation and New Creation fit together.

While *adam* is clearly not divine, he is created in the image and likeness of God and this points to *adam's* role as a sign of God's activity and presence in the life of the world. Insofar as we participate in *adam*, we too are entrusted with the profound role of reflecting this image of God in our manner of living. Being created in the image of God must guide our understanding of the command to 'fill the earth and subdue it' (Gen. 1.28). Holding together these two aspects of our creaturely vocation – being made in the image of God and being commanded to 'subdue' the earth – will prohibit our abuse of creation. The dominion commanded by God, this subduing of creation, cannot include a violent wielding of power. The command can only be understood as stewardship in the form of nurture, guidance and care.

In the description of the second half of the sixth day and the seventh day we find a new verbal detail: the definite article is added to the day's number. We do not notice this in English translations. The little word 'the' (Heb: *ha*) from this point on precedes the number of the day as it is mentioned. This is unlike each earlier day, and emphasizes *adam*'s status as height of the creation on the sixth day. It also points to the ascending order of Creation.

The addition of the article to the number of each day, along with the 'six-plus-one' literary pattern that shapes the whole account, introduces the seventh day as creation's true climax. *Adam* is indeed the apex of living things, but is not the main concern of the creation story. Here all roads lead to the seventh day, to the Sabbath. This day is God's blessing on, contemplation of and delight in the goodness of all God has wrought. The Sabbath is the true climax of God's creation.

Genesis 1 opened with a statement about God's action; it now closes with a statement about God's action. All of God's creative work is fulfilled here in the seventh day. This day contrasts with the other six days of creative activity in pointing to God's concluded labour. This divine rest is a key element of all of God's creative work, even above and beyond the creation of Adam.

Creation is entirely independent of human effort. It is a free gift of grace. As such, it shows us God's presence in creation in a way completely unlike our modern understandings of God. God is wholly outside of nature, and yet intimately tied to it, sanctifying it, hovering over it in blessing, remaining present to and with it. At creation, *adam* may seem to be the centre of his own world, but this is only because God has granted *adam* a privileged status. It is God's work of the seventh day that tips the reader off to this fact.

We in whom the first Adam rules assume that we ourselves are at the centre of our world. When we realize that we are not, we are indignant. But it is God who is at the centre. We can pretend all we want that this is not so, but that doesn't make it true. The fact that the tree of life is at the centre of the Garden of Eden and functions as a type of Cross makes this even clearer (2.9).[4] The Cross as the tree of life is, properly speaking, at the centre of the world, even though we seek to usurp its place.

If we claim to own its place, we all too easily make the world our plaything. And in modern times, this is what we have done: made God's good creation our toy box. If we are at the centre of our world, then our individual rights overpower communal relations. No wonder our environment sickens. No wonder racial, ethnic, sexual violence seems to reign. We have planted ourselves at the centre, at the place where the Tree of Life grows.

At the end of the Genesis creation story, after the expulsion of our first parents from the Garden of Eden, God first curses the serpent:

he will eat the dust of the ground (Gen. 3.14–15). God then curses Eve: even though she desires her husband, she will nevertheless endure the pain of his ruling over her, and yet having the joy of giving birth to and loving her children (3.16). Later, Mary, as the second Eve, will hear Simeon's words, which confirm this: even in her bearing and loving her Son. 'A sword will pierce your own soul, too' (Lk. 2.35).

God then casts the longest of curses on Adam. The final phrases are:

> By the sweat of your face
> you shall eat bread
> until you return to the ground,
> for out of it you were taken;
> you are dust,
> and to dust you shall return. (Gen. 3.19)

On Ash Wednesday, our foreheads are marked in the sign of the cross with the final words of Adam's curse. In the singsong first line of the eighteenth-century New England alphabet primer, 'In Adam's fall we sinnèd all'. What does this mean for us? We each harbour in our own being the first Adam. And yet we each in our baptism now also are recreated in the image of Christ, the second Adam. For us, that dust to which we return will be reformed into new bodies in the resurrection.

God's address in Genesis 1 is a foreshadowing of the calling of the People of Israel. This address creates the possibility of a relationship that is a type of the Body of Christ.[5] Being addressed by God brings us into relationship with each other and with Christ. This means that we do not come face to face with God apart from each other. Neither does the Church as the Body of Christ come into relationship with God apart from the people of the Promise, Israel.

As Christians we are grafted into the people of the Promise (cf Rom 11). Because God has already addressed us also with a marriage proposal, we cannot be silent. We must choose our response, either in rejection of God or in praise. God sits enthroned upon the praises of Israel (Ps. 22.3). Even so, Jesus reminds us that God does not need our praises in order to be God: even if we do not praise, the rocks would do so in our place (Lk. 19.37–40). We owe God thanks and praise, and yet even in our praise we cannot fully do Him homage: 'We could say more but we could never say enough ...' (*Sir.* 43.27). God's presence overflows and outspreads even our own praise and thanksgiving. But in our praise, we are assured of God's presence.

Questions for further reflection

- St Francis is known for his abiding care for both the poor and for animals. What does Genesis 1 say about this kind of passionate care for them? How might you embrace this kind of care in your own life?

- St Martin of Tours also cared deeply for the poor and taught what has become a classic tenet of the Christian faith – Jesus is fully human and fully God. How do we love God and neighbour in both the poor and creation?

- In an age when our environment has become sickened, how might Christians heed God's command in Genesis 1.28 to be stewards of creation?

2

Noonday: God's Presence in Angels of Light

Ye holy angels bright,
who wait at God's right hand,
or through the realms of light
fly at your Lord's command,
assist our song,
for else the theme
too high doth seem
for mortal tongue.

RICHARD BAXTER (1615–1691), 1681

In the very beginning of the story, we hear the Word that creates light. This Word grounds and establishes God's relationship with creation: God is with us. This relationship of uncompromised presence is a key theme of the Bible: 'Yet I am always with you; you hold me by my right hand' (Ps. 73.23). Throughout Scripture, one of the many ways in which God's presence comes to us is through His angels of light.

Angels in Scripture are very different from the angels we may be familiar with. Many of us will think of angels as plastic figurines with halos and wings that we use as decorations on our Christmas trees. There is nothing inherently wrong with this, if the figurines remind us of God's presence and make us thankful. But they have little in common with the biblical angels who mediate God's presence to us in light.

In the fifth century, St Augustine wondered how angels could hold such an important place in Scripture and yet not be mentioned among all the things God made in the first two chapters of Genesis. Literally everything under the sun, including the sun itself, is mentioned there as God's direct creation. But angels do not figure in the story anywhere. Augustine decided that, because angels are present throughout Scripture, and because they don't compete with God but serve him, they must be created beings. Augustine suggested that angels are to be found in the creation of the first day, at God's words 'Let there be light.' Angels are light; they dwell in light; they shed God's light. They are the light that illumines even though the creatures of the fourth day (the sun, moon, and stars) are not yet created. Because Satan disguises himself as an angel of light, Satan seems all the more terrifying than we might have thought (2 Cor. 11.14). Darkness, when disguised as light, becomes that much more attractive, and therefore that much more dangerous.

An elder in the Presbyterian church who was widely read in Christian history and Scripture and who was a faithful attender of adult education classes bristled when she heard that her hero John Calvin believed in angels. Why did this towering figure in her church tradition have such an interest in fanciful beings as angels?

'Because they are in the Bible,' I responded.

'Well, yes, that's true. But they seem so Catholic.'

Even someone as critical of the Roman Catholic Church as the sixteenth-century Reformer could not sweep aside the biblical reality of angels. Because he was committed to holding steadfastly to Scripture as guide to church doctrine and governance, he was committed to reading carefully also the texts where angels appear. This is just one of the many places in which the Protestant Reformation cry for 'Scripture alone' had a concrete impact on Calvin's interpretation of the Bible that aligned him with the Church's tradition. If we are to read the Bible seriously, we cannot ignore the reality of angels.

The word for 'angel' itself (Gk: *angelos*; Heb: *mal'akh*) means simply 'messenger'. A related word in Greek is *euangelion*, from which we derive our English words evangel, evangelical

and evangelist. The Greek word for 'promise' is also related
to its root. In bringing messages, angels often surprise and
frighten those to whom they appear. They also bring words of
comfort and promise.

We find angels throughout the Bible in both the Old and the
New Testaments. Angels announce God's naming of children
who will be important for the people of Israel and for the Church.
They declare God's victory over evil. Angels mediate God's
command, and commission humans for divine action. They are
the promised agents of God's judgement at the end of time. And
angels continually behold the face of God in heaven, for they
dwell in God's presence (Mt. 18.10). Because of this, they reflect
the glory of God's light.

Abraham at the Oaks of Mamre

While in Scripture angels often appear mysteriously as if out of
nowhere, sometimes they are far more ordinary. Sometimes they
are even described as though they could be humans. Scripture
indeed suggests that we Christians function as angels for each
other. We need to look out for opportunities to see each other
in this way: 'Do not neglect to show hospitality to strangers, for
by doing that some have entertained angels without knowing it'
(Heb. 13.2).

The story of Abraham and the visitors to his tent at the Oaks of Mamre is one place where angels come on the scene as though simply ordinary people. It is the LORD Himself who appears to Abraham on a hot afternoon, although He does this through angels. Abraham looks up and sees three visitors, described simply as 'men' (Heb: *anashim*). The only way the reader knows that these visitors are not mere mortals is that the chapter had just opened with the statement 'The LORD appeared to Abraham' (Gen. 18.1). So, the attentive reader knows that these three visitors somehow mediate the presence of God – even though the word 'angel' is not used, clearly their role is angelic: they bear a message and mediate the presence of the LORD.

This term, the LORD, points to the Divine Name. This Name itself is sometimes called the Tetragrammaton because it has four (*tetra*) letters (*grammata*). While the Name, the LORD, has already appeared in Genesis 2.4, it will later be dramatically revealed in Exodus 3. We will learn more about this in chapter 3. But here in Genesis 18, the Name simply appears in introducing the main character in the dialogue between Abraham and God-in-the-three-men in reassurance of the promise. After the three men ask where Sarah is, they seem to fade into the background of the narrative, not to reappear. Only one remains (18.10), who then confirms the promise that Sarah will bear a son, Isaac. This promise itself indicates the presence of the LORD to the people of Israel.

One of the most celebrated representations of this story in the history of art and iconography – 'The Hospitality of Abraham' by Russian Orthodox monk Andrei Rublev – trades on this ambiguity between humans and angels. This icon was written (icons are 'written', not 'painted') in the early fifteenth century and is on one level a rendering of the scene in Genesis 18. In Rublev's icon, though, Abraham's visitors are more than just ordinary humans. They have wings and halos, and represent the persons of the Holy Trinity, from left to right clockwise: Father, Son and Holy Spirit. Above the Son, we see what seems to be an Oak of Mamre, representing also the Tree of Life in the Garden of Eden. The Tree of Life in turn is understood throughout the history of Christian biblical interpretation to be a type of Christ and his cross.[6] To give a proper account of this icon is neither within my competence nor within the scope of this little book, but the icon itself is more than worthy of prayerful attention. It is at least noteworthy that Rublev presents this scene where the LORD appears to Abraham in the form of three men as angels who each represent the persons of the Trinity: God is with-us-in-relation, in humanity.

After Genesis 18 with this scene of the promise, the narrative then turns towards a truly theological and even ethical vision. Abraham for the first time becomes a moral agent: he pleads with God in a bargain over the future of the wicked city of Sodom (Gen. 18.22ff.). Abraham appeals to God's own righteousness in pleading for the salvation of the city, mediating God's own faithfulness: 'Far be it from you to do such a thing, to slay the righteous with the wicked, so that the righteous fare as the wicked! Far be that from you! Shall not the Judge of all the earth do what is just?' (Gen. 18.25). Abraham himself now represents God's presence and promise, seeming to be even more righteous than God Himself.

We find another artistic rendition inspired by biblical angels-as-humans in the African American gospel song 'We Are Climbing Jacob's Ladder'. This song is in its own right an icon of the strength of African slaves in holding on to the promise of God's presence even in their darkest hours. It embraces what has become one of the most evocative scenes in the Bible, in Genesis 28, wherein God encounters Jacob in a dream at Bethel, again mediated through angels. In this encounter, Jacob is crafted into a character in his own right. Here we enter another bend in the road along the way to the fulfilment of the promise of God's presence among the people of Israel.

Jacob's Dream at Bethel

Much as the encounter with the angels at Mamre was a turning point in the formation of Abraham's character, so now Jacob's vision of the angels at Bethel will shape his own identity. Jacob as a character in his own right comes to the fore at this point in the narrative. Previously, he had been overshadowed by his relationships with family: mother, father, brother. The fraught interactions between him and his brother Esau are for the moment behind him. Once a coddled mama's boy, Jacob becomes a man of substance in this encounter with the angels, and this biblical episode transforms his future.

In Genesis 28.10ff. Jacob finds a place to sleep. We have no idea where he is, and neither, apparently, does he. The narrator gives us no hint. It is described simply as somewhere between Beersheba and Haran. In other words, we are somewhere between the extreme south of the Israelite territory yet to come and the place where Abraham's family first stopped after leaving Ur of the Chaldeans. Because the family still has kin there(Gen. 11.31–32), Isaac has sent Jacob specifically there to look for a wife. The fact that Jacob is headed to his ancestral 'home' is integral to the plot for the development of the promise's confirmation.

This place is not mentioned as anything but an anonymous place, and is only named after Jacob's dream there (28.17–19): Jacob says it is the 'house of God' (Heb: *Beth-El*). Bethel itself has no specified geographical or historic importance thus far in the story, but it will after this episode.

Much earlier in the story, Abraham pitched his tent near this place. He built an altar there and invoked the name of the LORD. But this was not at Bethel itself (Gen. 12.8; 13.3). There is no reason either for us or for Jacob to expect God's encounter here, whether in a dream or any other kind of revelation. The stopover itself is apparently unplanned: 'He came to a certain place and stayed there for the night, because the sun had set.' Jacob does not call upon the LORD; he simply sleeps and, perchance, dreams. God is not summoned, and yet appears unexpectedly in Jacob's dream. The LORD, the God of Jacob's fathers, confirms the promises of land and descendants (v. 14).

In his dream, Jacob sees angels ascending to heaven and descending to earth on something like a ladder. The angels themselves seem to have no specific function on the ladder, other than their action of ascending and descending (28.12). The most important detail is that the LORD is somehow present, either on top of the ladder, or else beside Jacob (v. 13). What is most clear, though, is that it is the LORD who addresses Jacob, identifying Himself as the God of Abraham and Isaac. This is no anonymous God. This is a God with a history, who makes history by entering history.

We know that the appearance of God here is grace, because Jacob is amazed, unsuspecting, bowled over. The God of Jacob's father and grandfather is free to bless. At creation God freely pours out His grace in creating the world, and here God repeats His free promise of blessing on the covenant people. Grace that is not free is not really grace. It is wages earned (Rom. 4.4).

At this point we hear the LORD promise Jacob that He will be with him: 'I am with you and will keep you wherever you go, and I will bring you back to this land; I will not leave you until I have done what I promised you' (Gen. 28.15). God promises to be present throughout everything He has planned for Jacob and his children: torturous journeys, plenty and want, joys and sorrows. Even though Jacob leaves the land, God promises to be present, just as He will be as Jacob leaves for Egypt (46.4). There, too, God will meet Jacob through an angelic figure in a dream.

God's presence with Jacob, however, is not just a word of comfort at a time of generalized fear and insecurity. God's presence here is tied specifically to the fulfilling of His purposes for Jacob's future wanderings. God's presence will embrace protection and care. When Jacob awakes, his response is one of surprise at God's presence: 'Surely the LORD is in this place and I did not know it!' (Gen. 28.16). If he had known, he would not have treated it as a profane place, using it as a campground. But now he realizes that God's presence has made it a holy place, indeed the 'gateway of heaven' (28.17).

Christian interpreters have historically understood Jacob's description of this 'gateway of heaven' to be a type of Christ. Jesus says 'I am the door' (Jn 10.7; Rev. 3.20). Jesus himself is this gateway of heaven, a door opening our earthly reality to the divine presence. There is a sense in which we can even say that it is the Lord Jesus who stood beside Jacob at that ladder (v. 13).

The story continues. Jacob conducts a ritual of anointing the stone that had pillowed his head in the dream. He commemorates the revelation, acknowledging that God alone has made the profane place holy by His presence. This is apparently not a new ritual to Jacob, because he just performs it with no fanfare, no elaborate description. But now the place means something radically new: the God of Israel has opened the heavens.

Here Jacob becomes a Patriarch. God declares that Jacob will share in the promises of land and offspring, the two promises with which God blessed Jacob's father and grandfather, Isaac and Abraham, each in their own day. But this promise is not a static gift. It is not sealed in the present. It is a promise yet to be fulfilled. The promises of the entire Bible lean forward, into the future.

It should strike us as comforting to find that Jacob the Patriarch is no sterling example of character formation. He is a sneak, a cheat and a liar. But even this is no hurdle for God, who nevertheless chooses Jacob to be next in the line of patriarchs. Jacob becomes a leader and template for what God will make of the covenant people, but only because of God's grace, and not because of Jacob's merit. It is immaterial to God's grace who Jacob has been in the past. God is concerned more with Jacob's future than with his past.

Hagar and the Angel of the LORD

God works through angels to give promises even also to Gentiles, to those outside the covenant people of God (cf. especially Gen. 28.14). Angels give good news even to those who are of no special importance either to Israel or to the Church, even to those whose descendants will be set against the people of Israel. Even Hagar, the mother of Isaac's elder brother, the not-promised Ishmael, receives a promise through the mediation of an angel.

The promise to Hagar is a very unlikely promise indeed, a promise easily overlooked as we read Genesis. The angel who appears to Hagar says that God will bless and increase even the descendants of Ishmael. Even though Ishmael will be the elder who serves the younger, a flip in the usual social norm, he himself will receive his own blessing.

The fact that Hagar is described as an 'Egyptian' should not be lost on us. This word is repeated three times in each of the opening verses of Genesis 16, where we first meet her. 'Egyptian' is her designation again later in 21.9. The proper noun 'Egypt', of course, echoes throughout the Bible. Egypt is a place fraught with conflicting episodes in the story of Israel: lying and truth-telling, slavery and mastery, famine and feeding, assault and protection. The main role Egypt plays in the overarching story, however, is as threat to the people of Israel. And yet Hagar the Egyptian is blessed through an angel of the LORD, God of Israel.

As Abram's first son, Ishmael should have received the blessing normally due the first son. It is not yet clear at this point in the story, though, that this is the son who has been promised (Gen. 13.15–16; 15.5), or that the promised son will come specifically through Sarai. We only learn this later (Gen. 17.19; 18.10). But here in chapter 16, Sarai is getting impatient for a child, and she attempts to force the promise by arranging for a surrogate mother. She gives her Egyptian maidservant Hagar to Abram. After she sees that Hagar has conceived, however, Sarai becomes distressed, and treats Hagar harshly, to the point where Hagar finally flees.

And we now we come upon the desperate Hagar, pregnant and afraid, alone in the desert. This scene foretells her distress in chapter 21, when she will have been cast out, again due to Sarai's jealousy and anger. The first hint of blessing here in chapter 16 is that she is at a spring of water. A well becomes a blessing to Hagar again in 21.19. It would be an understatement to say that water was a rare and precious commodity in the Near East in biblical times, as it still is today. Here we come upon the first appearance of an angel of the LORD in the Bible (Gen. 16.7). It is striking that the first encounter we have with the angel of the LORD is in the context of the LORD's blessing a Gentile, indeed an Egyptian, moreover an Egyptian woman. These qualifications make her the lowest on the totem pole of social context.

The angel gives Hagar a promise that, even though secondary to Isaac's promise, will be grace-filled. The blessing includes making Ishmael's offspring an uncountable multitude (Gen. 16.10). This is somewhat like the blessing we heard in Genesis 13 and 15 about Isaac's future identity. Ishmael's blessing in Genesis 16 foretells the blessing in Genesis 21.12. Ishmael will be the father of a great people simply because he is a son of Abram: God is true to His word. In 16.11 the angel mediates God's blessing to Hagar.

As elsewhere in Scripture, names promise the future role of characters. God names the boy with a play on words that forecasts his future identity: 'You shall call his name Ishmael, for the LORD has given heed to your affliction' (Gen. 16.11). We find here another Hebrew pun that hides in English translation. The pun comes in the similarity of the name (*Yishmaʼel*: Ishmael) with the verb (*shamaʼ*; to heed or hear). The blessing also includes an assessment of the boy's character and future role in the narrative of Israel: 'He shall be a wild ass of a man, with his hand against everyone, and everyone's hand against him; and he shall live at odds with all his kin' (Gen. 16.12). God blesses even the one who is least likely to be favoured in any regard, the one who will set himself against the promise of God to his own kin.

One of the most remarkable things about Hagar at this point is that she 'named the LORD who spoke to her' (Gen. 16.13). She seems to be the first character in the Bible to give God a name: El-roi. Even though she gets the name 'wrong' (because the proper name for the God of Israel is the LORD), El-roi is her own name for God. And her name for the God who is for her is yet another play on words: a combination of the generic word for God (*El*) and the verb 'to see' (*ra'ah*). She has seen God and yet lives. Hagar the Egyptian knows that seeing God is a double-edged sword, an experience which only a very few in the Bible actually survive.

The fact that she is Ishmael's mother and yet receives such mercy makes the story all the more remarkable. Ishmael is no neutral figure in the rest of Scripture. He will become a threat to the people of the promise, and yet that blessing is given only for the sake of God's faithfulness to Abraham (Gen. 21.13). This angel mediates God's blessing even on Hagar, and her son.

Angels in the Nativity Story

Abraham's visitors, Jacob's ladder, Hagar's well: these are, of course, not the only places in Scripture where we find God's angels of light. Angels visit Joseph and then Mary; they meet them in dreams, too, especially in the Nativity stories. They mediate God's commands, confer God's promises, declare God's demand of our obedience. As they fulfil these tasks, the narrative moves us forward toward the fulfilment of the promised presence of God in the birth and protection of Emmanuel, God-with-us the Light of the World.

The first angel to protect the child Jesus appears to Joseph in a dream after he has discovered that Mary is 'with child'. In this first dream, Joseph hears the angel reveal the origin, identity and purpose of this otherwise shameful and shaming event. How could this have happened when they have not 'known' each other? After having decided to release Mary secretly from her promise to him, Joseph hears an anonymous angel address him in a dream: 'Joseph, son of David, do not be afraid to take Mary as your wife, for the child conceived in her is from the Holy Spirit' (Mt. 1.20). A few verses later, we find that Joseph follows through on the angel's command, and takes Mary as his wife. Without this angel's appearance, and Joseph's obedience to the charge, those of us who are Gentiles would remain strangers to the covenant. We would still be without Emmanuel, God-with-us. We would be indeed left orphans (Jn 14.18), strangers to the covenant and in darkness (1 Peter 2:9), without God in the world. (Eph. 2.12).

Later, another anonymous angel appears to Joseph and instructs him to flee to Egypt in order to protect the family from Herod's murderous plan to destroy the infant. Herod perceives this baby to pose a threat to his own power. He is frightened enough to scheme to eliminate any child who would fit the profile. Herod plans to search out this little one, proclaimed by the (Gentile!) Magi to be King of the Jews (Mt 2.13).

Jesus, the King of the Jews, takes on the identity and role of his own people, Israel. In the story of Joseph and Mary's flight to Egypt, Jesus mirrors his ancestor, Moses, who was skilfully protected from a similar plot. Pharaoh, threatened by the Hebrew people, sought to eliminate them by ordering the murder of all of their infant boys (Ex 1:22). In the Gospel according to Matthew, an angel will appear to Joseph again and instruct him to take the family back to Israel (Mt 2:19). Jesus is brought out of hiding in Egypt, again taking on the identity of Israel. He will continue to play the role of his people Israel and take on their identity throughout his life, death and resurrection.

The story of Herod's murderous plan to eliminate Jesus is not detailed at any great length in the New Testament (cf. Mt 2.16–18). However, it has fascinated Christians, particularly through medieval and Renaissance painting. The story has even become a day of special commemoration in the liturgical calendar: the Holy Innocents, 28 December. Is this commemoration based on a sense of compassion for the parents who lost their boys in that land, at that time? Is it meant to shape us in love of God and love of neighbour? On the surface, it may seem nothing but a horrible reminder of our deep inhumanity. But tragedy can function another way too, especially in Scripture.

The Holy Innocents and Ours

In 2012, in a sleepy little New England town in the north-eastern United States, we witnessed a carnage that shook the entire nation.

In a shooting spree, a total of twenty-eight people lost their lives. Twenty of them were small children at school and play. It would be impossible to capture in words our collective grief and horror.

The shooting was just two weeks before the commemoration of the Holy Innocents. During Holy Eucharist on the Sunday after the massacre, a local priest prayed, in addition to the collect for that week, the collect for the Feast of the Holy Innocents:

> We remember today, O God, the slaughter of the holy innocents of Bethlehem by King Herod. Receive, we pray, into the arms of your mercy all innocent victims; and by your great might frustrate the designs of evil tyrants and establish your rule of justice, love, and peace; through Jesus Christ our Lord, who lives and reigns with you, in the unity of the Holy Spirit, one God, for ever and ever. Amen. (BCP, p. 238)

This collect enfolded the suffering of those little children and their families into the larger story of the Gospel: the overcoming of the world's evil. The collect held these children's lives and deaths as linked to Jesus' own, and therefore also to his resurrection. The prayer cried to God for these dear children and all others who suffer to be gathered into the arms of God's mercy.

But there the correspondence between King Herod's massacre and the Sandy Hook massacre ends. Yes, blessing was poured out for the world in the Holy Innocents of Jesus' day. Yes, their deaths protected the Christ Child. Even so, most of us find it difficult to see the hand of God at work in history in that way. How would the Hebrew mothers have felt at their loss?

But at Sandy Hook, these little children seem to have suffered apart from the saving work of Herod's Holy Innocents. This event only begins tentatively to be redeemed insofar as we are able to see the ancient Holy Innocents as a type of our Holy Innocents of Sandy Hook. In this way, we might begin to embrace our own Holy Innocents of Sandy Hook as angels who mediate the presence of God in light. This does not lessen the tragedy or their pain at all. Which mother or father wants their child to play this role? We must not ever think of uttering the horrific excuse that God 'wanted them home', as some glibly suggested. The horror remains seeringly painful. But if we can frame the horror within the larger narrative of God's love poured out in Jesus, which was a horror in its own right, we might be able to endure such innocent suffering. Not to make an excuse for it, but simply to endure it.

The world seems bent on violence in so many ways. We have a choice to make between life and death. We can accept the marriage proposal or we can reject it. We can choose to belong to God, or we can choose to follow other gods. Anything that crowds out God from the centre of our devotion, anything that separates us from God, anything that hinders our heeding God's promises and walking in His paths, binds us in darkness. And this can happen even in the noon of the day, when the light of the sun is at its strongest and most brilliant, when we should be best able to see. And so we pray for peace.

Even in our imprisonment to violence and suffering, Christ is present. He is present among us here in our darkest place in his crucifixion. Stretching out his arms on the hard wood of the cross, he is present. As Jacob says: 'Truly God is in this place and I did not know it. Truly this is the gateway to heaven' (Gen. 28.16). It is only in the power of the cross that we dare even whisper into the deepest of human sorrow: God is present.

The Christian life is one long stretching forward toward the presence of God, when darkness will be vanquished, when sorrow will be no more. Paul says, 'I press on toward the goal for the prize of the heavenly call of God in Christ Jesus' (Phil. 3.14). God's promises lean the Christian forward into the future. This is the essence of Christian hope. It looks beyond the cross, out of the empty tomb, and toward the horizon of Jesus' return in glory. Then will God be unrestrainedly present in light and peace and joy. This is the Christian hope, even in darkness that can paradoxically seem to overcome us at the noon of the day.

Questions for further reflection

- Do we see angels continuing to function in the devotion and prayers of the life of the Church?

- Do we find angels in our own lives? How do we know they are angels? How do we respond to them?
- What word do we bring (as angels ourselves) to a culture for which hope in God is considered obsolete or naïve or even illogical?

3

Afternoon: God's Presence in the Divine Name

Who is this God Who Addresses Us?

We know from the previous chapter that the God of the Bible is not a generic deity, but a God of place and time and people and history. This God has a name that He shares with His people, Israel. It is a name that pinpoints God's identity. Related to the verb 'to be', the Divine Name itself indicates God's presence: the One Who Is, the One Who is There, the One Who is Present, the One Who Will Be.

We have also seen that throughout the Bible God gives names to people through angels. These names show the recipient's identity and future role in the story of redemption. But God's name itself does not come through an angel, or even a prophet, or representative of any kind. God is the one who announces the Divine Name, God's own self-designation. In so far as this God tells us His name, who He is apart from how He is for us, He relinquishes an element of control. This is what it means to know someone's name, to be introduced to someone: we have a small degree of power in our relationship with that person. But God chooses all the same anyway to give His name to Moses and therefore also to us. Here again we find a God who is free to be who He is, free to give His name to whom He chooses.

There are many names for God in the Old Testament, but two of the most common ones are Elohim and YHWH. These are most often translated respectively 'God' and 'LORD' in English. The Divine Name, as mentioned earlier, is sometimes referred to as the Tetragrammaton, from the Greek for 'four letters'.[7]

God's Presence, Fire and the Divine Name

In Exodus 3, we read a story in which an angel of the LORD appears to Moses in the light of God's presence on Horeb (in another tradition known as Sinai). Later in Exodus the Law will be given on this mountain. This Law will claim the people of Israel and will cement their covenant relationship with the LORD. In the burning bush, an angel appears, and introduces to Moses the presence of the LORD. This is one of the most powerful and identity-changing episodes in the entire Old Testament, rivalling the giving of the Law.

As Exodus 3 opens, we find Moses guarding his Midianite father-in-law's sheep. Like Jacob at Bethel, Moses is not described as seeking a religious experience or encounter with God. He is simply described as a shepherd. This, of course, was a common occupation in the Ancient Near East. Throughout the Bible shepherds represent leadership, guidance and protection. Many of the great leaders and prophets of Israel are referred to as shepherds. Jesus himself will take on this title to describe his own vocation (esp. Jn 10).

The fact that Moses' father-in-law is a Midianite is a detail not to be overlooked. Not only are Midianites Gentiles (not belonging to the covenant people of Israel), but they are the very people who were traitors to Israel. We remember that earlier in the biblical story it was a group of Midianites who first rescued Joseph from the well into which his own brothers had thrown him, only then to sell him into bondage in Egypt (Gen. 37.28). This treachery leads subsequently to the slavery of the Hebrews in Egypt. And yet out of their slavery in Egypt, the LORD hears Israel's cry. In order to lead them out of their sufferings, the LORD chooses Moses,

the shepherd of the Midianite priest. To put it mildly, Moses
has a complicated relationship with his own people, the
Hebrews.

Even so, the narrator emphasizes that Moses is indeed
a Hebrew and is of the tribe of Levi. The detail is strangely
noted: his lineage is traced through both of his parents – not
only his father but also his mother, just in case we did not catch
it the first time (Exod. 2.1). This is one of the places in the
Bible where we note the importance of tracing Jewish ancestry
through the mother. Moses is definitely and undeniably from
the house of Levi; he is not only a Hebrew, he is of the priestly
tribe. Levi is, in religious terms, the most important of all the
tribes of Israel.

As mentioned in the previous chapter, in the 'original' Holy
Innocents narrative Pharaoh becomes afraid of the strength
of the Hebrews (Exod. 1.8–22). He plots to kill all the Hebrew
baby boys. But through the teamwork of Moses' own mother
(a Hebrew) and Pharaoh's daughter (not merely a Gentile, but
an Egyptian!) Moses himself is saved (2.3–10). Notice who
names this Hebrew hero: an Egyptian woman. In another
naming pun, Moses' future role in guiding the Hebrews to
freedom is announced. Pharaoh's daughter unwittingly makes
a play on words in Hebrew: she gives him the name Moses
(*Moshe*), because, as she said, 'I drew him [*mashah*] out of the
water' (2.10b). That an Egyptian would make a play on words

in Hebrew, a language not her own, to indicate the future role of this Hebrew baby who will throw off the yoke of Egypt is a delightfully ironic twist!

Moses' name points forward to his role in leading his people through the Red Sea and also picks up the earlier theme of God's rescuing Noah from the waters of the flood (Gen. 6–9). This story itself picks up the earlier instance of the same theme: God separates the dry land from the seas (Gen. 1.9).[8] Rescuing from the waters of death will become important later in the New Testament.

Thus Moses is protected from the Egyptians. Ironically, this future Hebrew hero who will throw off the yoke of the oppressor Egypt is raised, nurtured and protected in Pharaoh's own home (Exod. 2.10).

As a grown man, Moses intervenes in a deadly fight between an Egyptian and a Hebrew, and inadvertently kills the Egyptian (2.11–12). In this scene the narrator notes, in a further detail not to be overlooked, that the Hebrew being beaten by this Egyptian is 'one of [Moses'] own kinfolk' (2.11). The next day Moses gets embroiled in a fight between two other Hebrews. They in turn make public his murder of the Egyptian the previous day, which had apparently been until this point a secret (2.14). Pharaoh himself then sets out to kill Moses, who flees to Midian, as we have seen. There, he is taken to be an Egyptian (not a Hebrew!) by the son of the priest of Midian (Exod. 2.19). Moses marries the priest's daughter, who of course is a Gentile. In a further twist of irony, Moses names his son Gershom, which is related to the word for 'alien' in Hebrew.

Why are these details important? They emphasize a question that all along we have been pondering: Who is this Moses? To whom does he really belong? Is he a Hebrew? An Egyptian? A Midianite? He has allegiance to all of these peoples: to the oppressor Gentiles of Egypt, to the oppressed Hebrews needing to be freed from Egypt, and to the traitorous Midianites with whom he is now kin. The most important question, of course, is this: what is the nature of Moses' relationship to the God of Israel? It seems that Moses does not point easily to the identity of God, but that God has to break through Moses' own conflicted identity to reveal Himself.

Fire that Burns but Does Not Consume

Our story in Exodus 3 where the Divine Name is revealed to Moses from out of the burning bush is yet another point in Scripture where we find God's absolute freedom to make His presence known in light. There is no particular reason given in the story why God must reveal His Name to Moses. There appears to be no constraint on God's part whatsoever. Moses, who at present has only sketchy allegiance to this God, holds no power in the relationship. This Moses, part-Hebrew, part-Egyptian, part-Midianite, simply asks God His name. And Moses does not ask out of mere curiosity – his question comes as a response to God's prior self-identification in 3.5–6 as 'the God of Abraham, Isaac, and Jacob', and to God's charge of Moses to lead the people out of Egypt (3.13, 16).

An angel of the LORD – again, not a generic angel, but one identified as a messenger of the LORD – appears to Moses in a 'flame of fire' out of a bush (Exod. 3.2). It is the *angel* who appears in the fire, not the LORD. Again we find an angel mediating God's presence in light. The oddest thing about this fire is that it blazes in the bush, but does not burn it up: the fire does not 'consume' the bush. This strange burning-but-not-burning-up bush grabs Moses' attention. He turns aside to examine this odd thing. When the LORD sees that Moses has turned aside, God (*Elohim*) calls to Moses by name: 'Moses, Moses!' God initiates a dialogue with Moses that will peak at the giving of the Divine Name – a dialogue which will continue to Moses' dying day.

Moses' response to God – 'Here I am!' (*hinneni*) – is a not-uncommon phrase in the Old Testament. It is a response that indicates attentiveness, readiness and eagerness on the part of the speaker. We find it three times on the lips of Abraham at the near-sacrifice of Isaac in Genesis 22. In that episode, Abraham first responds with the same phrase, 'Here I am!',

at God's calling his name (v. 1), a second time when the boy
Isaac asks where the lamb for the sacrifice is (v. 7), and a third
time when the angel stays ultimately his hand from slaying
the boy (v. 11). The emphasis is on Abraham's eagerness to
obey even this horrible command as well as his obedience
at the release from it. We also hear this phrase on the lips of
the young boy Samuel in 1 Samuel 3 as he repeatedly answers
what he perceives (mistakenly) to be Eli's call in the night.

In Exodus 3.4, God initiates the dialogue with Moses. God
knows Moses by name and calls out to him. Yet Moses seems
not to know God, much less what Moses' own role is to be
among God's people. After God introduces Himself as the God
(*Elohei*) of Abraham, Isaac and Jacob, He then declares in three
short statements that He has taken pity on His people. He has
'observed their misery'. He has 'heard their cry'. He 'knows their
sufferings' (v. 7). Because of this, God has come down to deliver
them from the hand of the Egyptians, and has chosen Moses to
be his fill-in.

But this seems not to satisfy Moses' curiosity. He assumes
that the people will know who this God is, even though
Moses himself apparently does not. God has already given
the lineage by which His history with this people is traced: He
is the God of Abraham, Isaac and Jacob. It seems Moses does
not know this history. Moses suggests that the people will
need some sort of authorization from God for them to pay

attention to him (v. 13). How will he convince them to follow him? By whose name will Moses command any authority?

The LORD God

At this point, God gives Moses a verbal description, a preview or advance sketch, of what the name will reveal about God's identity: 'God said to Moses, "I AM WHO I AM."' He said further, 'Thus you shall say to the Israelites, "I AM has sent me to you"' (Exod. 3.14).'I AM WHO I AM' can be translated also as 'I will be who I will be' or even 'I will bring into being what I will bring into being.' This God is present, is presence, and is being present as bringing into being. The Divine Name soon to be revealed will be linked openly with 'the God of Abraham, Isaac, and Jacob' (Exod. 3.15a) and with the One who called creation into being at the beginning of the Bible.

This God who self-identifies as 'being there' is not a generic presence. This God chooses to be present among a specific people, at a specific time, in a specific place. And yet this God's presence is not mired in that past. God's proper name is given into a specific context: the Exodus from Egypt. Other nations choose names for their own gods, but the God of Israel reveals His own name. This is Israel's God, who will bring the Israelites up out of bondage for the purpose of worship.

At this point Moses' response is not as eager as it had been earlier in verse 4, when he responded 'Here I am!' Now Moses wants to know 'Who am I that I should go to Pharaoh and bring the Israelites out of Egypt?' (v. 11). 'Who am I …?' indeed. If we were still wondering about Moses' relationship to Israel, his response here only drives it home: 'Who am I …?' or maybe better yet, 'Just leave me alone!'

In dialogue with God, Moses does not call the Hebrews 'your people'. God had referred to them in 3.7 as 'my people', so why wouldn't Moses refer to them when speaking to God as 'your people'? Instead, Moses refers to them as though at a remove, as though he were not one of them. He calls them simply 'Israelites'. And at 3.13 he asks about their hypothetical response to his claim to having been called by God. 'But Moses said to God, "If I come to the Israelites and say to them, 'The God of *your* ancestors has sent me to you,' and they ask me, 'What is his name?' what shall I say to them?"' The nature of Moses' relationship to God's people remains in question. Rather than instant clarification at this revelation of the LORD in dialogue with Moses at the burning bush, all we find is slowly dissipating mist.

Moses accepts his call only with a reluctance that anticipates the reactions of the classic prophets whom we will meet later in

Scripture: Isaiah ('"Woe is me …!"' [Isa. 6.5]); Jeremiah ('"… I am only a boy!"' [Jer. 1.6]) and Jonah ('Jonah set out to flee … from the presence of the LORD' [Jon. 1.3).

Moses gives three objections. The first we have heard: 'who am I …?' (Exod. 3.11). The second is basically a 'who are you?' (Exod. 3.13). The third is a question about the people themselves ('What if they do not believe me or listen to me?' Exod. 4.1). This comes after the Divine Name is revealed and the whole plan is laid out for Moses (Exod. 3.18–22). Even after Moses is given the Name, he invokes a hypothetical situation: 'what if …?' (4.1). It seems, then, that his reluctance is not tied directly to his ignorance of God's identity, but to his own fear and trembling.

The transformation in the relationship between God and Moses begun in this dialogue establishes Moses' understanding of his own vocation among the people of God. Moses' call shapes his understanding of God's relationship with His people, his own role before God and his own role among the people.

Moses' question regarding his own identity ('Who am I …?') is answered by God's promise of His presence and protection ('I will be with you …' [3.12]). This is a verbal hint at God's self-description as presence in verse 14: 'God said to Moses, "I AM WHO I AM."' God says further, 'Thus you shall say to the Israelites, "I AM has sent me to you."' At the Divine Name to be revealed at verse 15, we hear:

God also said to Moses, 'Thus you shall say to the Israelites,
"The LORD [YHWH], the God of your ancestors, the God
of Abraham, the God of Isaac, and the God of Jacob, has sent
me to you": This is my name forever, and this my title for all
generations.' (Exod. 3.15)

The name, verbally akin to the verb 'to be', is the third time in
this dialogue with Moses that we find God's identity revealed
in address and presence, each in crescendo from the previous.

Even while the Divine Name is a new name for the reader,
the God it names is the same God of the covenant to the
patriarchs and the God of creation. As early as Genesis 2.4
in the story of creation, the narrator simply drops the Divine
Name for the reader, but it is only in Exodus that Moses
himself learns God's Name in an I–thou relationship of
address and response. And yet it is at this address that the
LORD appears to Moses as a free agent and remains free.
God is not constrained or compelled to address Moses. God's
appearing is pure grace, sheer gift.

God's name is one with God's creative presence. Nothing
comes into the range of God's presence and stays the same.
As we saw in God's encounter with Abraham at the Oaks of
Mamre, and with Jacob in his dream, which changed their
role and purpose in the story of their people, so now God's
encounter with Moses sets him on a new path. God assures

Moses that He will be present and, even while unconstrained by this promise, will bring the people to freedom from slavery.

Freedom for Worship

God's presence will be accompanied by a sign: Moses together with Israel (the verb is a second person plural form: something like 'y'all' in colloquial speech of the southern United States) will worship God on that very mountain. This formerly estranged part-Egyptian part-Israelite with allegiance to the Midianites is now commissioned to lead God's people out of Egypt. And God will be with this Moses.

How striking that Israel's freedom is wrought not simply for the people's relief from suffering. Their liberation is for the purpose of worship of and praise to their Liberator. Israel's freedom from slavery in Egypt is found only in a relationship marked by worship. Israel's God who is present has addressed them and has introduced Himself by name. This worship is Israel's work, its office, its vocation, its purpose. It is a service that truly and finally sets Israel free from slavery.

O God, the author of peace and lover of concord, to know you is eternal life and to serve you is perfect freedom: Defend

us, your humble servants, in all assaults of our enemies; that
we, surely trusting in your defence, may not fear the power of
any adversaries; through the might of Jesus Christ our Lord.
Amen. (Morning Prayer Collect for Peace, BCP, p. 99)

It should not be lost on us that the words for 'worship', 'service'
and 'work' are the same in Hebrew. Yet even here, Israel's
worship will be a truly free response to its truly free Redeemer.
There is no sense that this 'sign' of its worship will be a response
of payment for services rendered. Israel's slavery to its Liberator
is not a *do ut des*, a form of control by God on Israel. Rather,
the sign of God's presence with Moses emphasizes Israel's true
freedom. 'Say to [Pharaoh] ... Let my people go that they may
worship me ...' (Exod. 7.16; 8.1). The sign will be in Israel's
freedom to serve their God in worship and praise. God is
present specifically as Redeemer and Liberator of Israel from
slavery in Egypt, and thus is the One to whom all worship and
service are due.

Idolatry and the Presence of God: the Golden Calf

In Exodus 32 we read the story of the Golden Calf, where Aaron
leads the people into apostasy. Even there, God is present, but

not in a comforting sense. We do find God's presence in light, but this light is not cheery. It is not the light of revelation as we saw in the fire that burned but did not burn up the bush. Here we find God's presence in light that terrifies the people. God's wrath burns and is ready to consume them. Moses' own anger burns hot and breaks forth as he destroys the tablets of the Law:

> As soon as he came near the camp and saw the calf and the dancing, Moses' anger burned hot, and he threw the tablets from his hands and broke them at the foot of the mountain. (Exod. 32.19)

God's presence will require something new – not so much a mediator as a buffer. This is indicated in part by the angel God will send at the end of the story, serving as protector for the people and helper for Moses.

Disgusted with their breach of fidelity, God expels the people from the holy site. God again refers to the people as though they were Moses' people, not His own, shaking off possession and responsibility. 'The LORD said to Moses, "Go, leave this place, you and the people whom *you* have brought up out of the land of Egypt"' (Exod. 33.1). Even in His burning anger, however, God remains steadfast in His promise to the patriarchs: '... go to the land of which I swore to Abraham, Isaac, and Jacob, saying, "To your descendants I will give it"' (Exod. 33.1). Even while God's promise is firm, God's presence among them on the journey is denied them. In His stead, God sends an angel to protect them as though from His own wrath.(Exod. 33.2).

God's distance from his people at this point will be a blessing rather than a curse: 'I will not go up among you, or I would consume you' (Exod. 33.3). God's absence is a mercy, because God's presence would be a threat. Why? God again calls the Israelites 'a stiff-necked people' and repeats the earlier statement that His presence would consume them (33.5). His presence on the journey would not be a comfort, but potentially lethal. Even here, though, God shows mercy in promising to be absent: God's absence is blessing and not curse. But this is only because of the people's infidelity, not because of God's identity. Normally, God's presence is blessing. But when we sin, it is God's absence that is mercy.

The people take up their own freedom to reject God, a freedom that is in fact slavery to idols of their own making. In their impatience at what they take to be Moses' delay on Sinai, they demand that Aaron help them make gods of their own. Aaron willingly consents. He tells them to take off the gold jewellery that they had plundered from the Egyptians, fashions it into a golden calf and introduces the animal to them: 'These are your gods, O Israel, who brought you up out of the land of Egypt!' (Exod. 32.4).[9] This was earlier the self-designation of the LORD: the One who brought them up out of the land of Egypt.

But while the golden calf is made with a 'graving tool' (Exod. 32.4), the Law of the LORD had been written on stone with the very 'finger of God' (Exod. 31.18).

Even though it was Aaron's doing, the LORD passes the blame to Moses. The blame game here recalls the similar conversation in Eden for the disobedience of Adam and Eve. Here too disobedience and sin mark the dialogue as they did there. The LORD usually refers to the people as His own, as He did at Moses' call:

> Then the LORD said, 'I have observed the misery of *my* people who are in Egypt; I have heard their cry on account of their taskmasters. Indeed, I know their sufferings ...' (Exod. 3.7)

But here the LORD passes them off to Moses as *his* people: 'The LORD said to Moses, "Go down at once! *Your* people, whom *you* brought up out of the land of Egypt, have acted perversely"'(Exod. 32.7).

The LORD has entrusted the people to Moses and they are now his responsibility. While it was the people who had requested gods, Aaron is the one to blame. Even so, it is Moses who intercedes with the Lord on behalf of this 'stiff-necked people' (Exod. 32.9). Here, Moses plays the role of Abraham who interceded on behalf of the wicked Sodom (Gen. 18).

As Abraham there, so now Moses stands in the breach for the people and reminds the LORD of His own promise:

> Why should the Egyptians say, 'It was with evil intent that he brought them out to kill them in the mountains, and to consume them from the face of the earth?' Turn from your fierce wrath; change your mind and do not bring disaster on your people. Remember Abraham, Isaac, and Israel, your servants, how you swore to them by your own self, saying to them, 'I will multiply your descendants like the stars of heaven, and all this land that I have promised I will give to your descendants, and they shall inherit it forever.' (Exod. 32.12–13)

Like Israel, the Church also is given the choice to embrace or to reject God. The decision is ours. The decision to choose a not-God, however, is a decision which is not free. Such a decision only jeopardizes our relationship with the LORD, which is the source of our life and our freedom. But in the morning of the Resurrection, on the eighth day we will know the LORD. We will encounter Him in relationship. We will come face to face with the LORD, and know His identity. We will be the LORD's, and the LORD will be present to us in the Name Jesus. And we will hear the Name of Jesus which we heard in the Divine Name revealed to Moses in Exodus 3 which echoes throughout Scripture and even now today:

Therefore my people shall know my name; therefore in that day they shall know that it is I who speak; here am I. (Isa. 52.6)

Questions for further reflection

- What does the verse from Isaiah – 52.6 – above tell us about the relationship between knowing God's name, hearing God's address and finding God's presence?
- Can you think of a time when God seemed absent from you but, looking back, you can see this as mercy?
- Does knowing God's Name require protecting God's Name? What, then, about the Name of Jesus?

4

Evening: God's Presence in the Name of Jesus

It is not physical beauty nor temporal glory nor the brightness of light dear to earthly eyes, nor the sweet melodies of all kinds of songs, nor the gentle odour of flowers, and ointments and perfumes, nor manna or honey, nor limbs welcoming the embraces of the flesh; it is not these I love when I love my God. Yet there is a light I love, and a food, and a kind of embrace when I love my God – a light, voice, odour, food, embrace of my innerness, where my soul is floodlit by light which space cannot contain, where there is sound that time cannot seize, where there is a perfume which no breeze disperses, where there is a taste for food no amount of eating can lessen, and where there is a bond of union that no satiety can part. That is what I love when I love my God.

ST AUGUSTINE, CONFESSIONS, 10.6

Jesus is that light we love, a light that will never be extinguished. He is the illumination caused by the shining of light. He is the light by which we see light (Ps 36:9). Jesus is the Word who spoke light into being. Jesus himself is that very light.

> In the beginning was the Word, and the Word was with God, and the Word was God. He was in the beginning with God. All things came into being through him, and without him not one thing came into being. What has come into being in him was life, and the life was the light of all people. The light shines in the darkness, and the darkness did not overcome it. (Jn 1.1–5)

This passage links creation in the past with the present of our lives, and folds them both into the future promise when all will be light. Jesus is the Word who was God, who spoke at Creation in the beginning. He is the agent of God's creation. He himself is the light that darkness does not and will not overcome, not even on the cross.

We often associate the images linking light and Jesus with the Gospel according to John and its sibling traditions. But it did not originate there. We find it in the earliest of Christian writings: St Paul's.

> For it is the God who said, 'Let light shine out of darkness,' who has shone in our hearts to give the light of the knowledge of the glory of God in the face of Jesus Christ. (2 Cor. 4.6)

Paul is doing more here than just referring to Scripture. In fact, Paul presents himself as quoting: '*For it is the God who said ...*' But he alters the words, as he does from time to time when he quotes Scripture. The question is: why? What is he trying to say? Surely Paul knows his Scripture. Genesis tells us: 'Then God said, "Let there be light." And there was light' (1.3). But Paul rephrases. God's impersonal command creating the light verb 'to be', 'Let there be ...', becomes in Paul's words an impersonal command giving power to the light: 'Let light shine ...' The light, says Paul, already performs the task it has been created to do: it shines. And it shines not on the darkness nor into the darkness as though from outside. It shines out of the darkness, as though from within the darkness. The light is active even from within the darkness in which dwell, shining as though outward. The light dwells even with us.

In the first chapter of Genesis, the light simply is. It exists. Here for Paul, though, the light God creates shines in a specific place, for a specific purpose. It is not any generic light. It is not simply the light of general wisdom or intelligence or discernment. The light that God commissions to shine out of darkness is tied to a specific knowledge. And what is this knowledge? Paul says that it is the knowledge of the glory of God in the face of Jesus Christ. This light is tied to a person, whose identity is tied in turn to the glory of God. The one who created light is the one who later will tell us that he himself is light, this Jesus. And that light is the very presence or 'face' of God.

Paul's phrasing in 2 Corinthians 4 shapes the way we understand Jesus' presence among us. Yes, Jesus is light in our darkness. But notice: Paul does not say that the light shines into the darkness, as though to scatter it, dispel it, or even overcome it. This is more like John 1.5. For Paul, here the light shines *out* of the darkness. This means that even from in the midst of our darkness, even *from within* our darkness, the light of Christ is strong enough to shine. But how can light shine *out of darkness* if it is not already there in the first place? Even within darkness, the defining reality is not the darkness itself. The light of Christ shines outward even from within there. That light gives us the knowledge of the glory of God. We have that knowledge in the person of Jesus.

In the Bible, the glory of God is more than just power and illumination. It is the very presence of God. And that presence of God is Jesus himself, whose fleshly face we behold. But very few characters in the Bible are allowed to see God and live. Moses spoke with God face to face as with a friend (Exod. 33.11). And as we read, Hagar, the Gentile mother of Ishmael, was allowed to see God's face (Gen. 16.13). But we know this is not the norm, and others who are allowed this privilege are few.

We, however, are invited to look on Jesus' merciful face. 'And we all, with unveiled face, beholding the glory of the Lord, are being changed into his likeness from one degree of glory to another; for this comes from the Lord who is the Spirit' (2 Cor. 3.18). Beholding Jesus' face does not destroy us. It transforms us. The glory of God shapes us into his likeness as a potter would transform a lump of muddy clay into a useful pot – maybe even a beautiful pot!

In the previous chapter, we reflected on the Divine Name revealed in Exodus 3. That name, YHWH, falls out of use in the New Testament. Here we are met by the emergence of the name Jesus. Even here, though, Jesus' name does not burst on the scene in the flames of revelation as abruptly as did YHWH in Exodus 3.15. It slowly comes to be whispered as Mary coos to her baby. Joseph, the guardian of the Lord, first learns the baby's name and its significance in his dream. There the angel promises: '[Mary] will bear a son, and you are to name him Jesus [*yeshua*], for he will save [*yasha*] his people from their sins' (Mt. 1.21). In the name 'Jesus' and its verbal root 'to save' we find yet another naming play on words. The name 'Jesus' gives us a foretaste of the baby's identity and vocation. He is Saviour.

Jesus declares that he is the Light of the World. We find throughout Scripture that Jesus' self-identification with light is linked also to life, healing and forgiveness. Jesus refuses to condemn the woman caught in adultery. In this he announces her own identity: forgiven. Jesus then proclaims his own identity: 'I am the light of the world. Whoever follows me will never walk in darkness but will have the light of life' (Jn 8.12, 21–24, 28).

Later, at the story of the healing of the man born blind in John 9, Jesus again declares himself to be light. 'As long as I am in the world, I am the light of the world' (Jn 9.5). In the earlier story, the light refuses to condemn, but forgives. This time the light heals. Jesus restores sight to the blind man. The way he does this points us to the Creation story, whether intentionally or not. The Light of the World creates light (vision) for the man with no vision by using mud, much as God created *adam* from mud (*adamah*) in Genesis 2.7.

Light

Jesus identifies himself with the God of Israel in the image of light, but what does this light do? It helps us see where we are going: 'Jesus said to them, "The light is with you for a little longer. Walk while you have the light, so that the darkness may not overtake you. If you walk in the darkness, you do not know where you are going"' (Jn 12.35). It assures us that we will not walk in darkness but 'will have the light of life' (Jn 8.12). This light is truth and life, and it conquers all darkness: 'The light shines in the darkness, and the darkness did not overcome it' (Jn 1.5). Light judges by exposing whatever prefers to hide in the darkness.

And this is the judgement, that the light has come into the world, and people loved darkness rather than light because their deeds were evil. For all who do evil hate the light and do not come to the light, so that their deeds may not be exposed.

But those who do what is true come to the light, so that it may be clearly seen that their deeds have been done in God. (Jn 3.19–21)

At the story of the raising of Lazarus, Jesus contrasts the ability to see and walk during the day with the stumbling that comes during the night: 'Jesus answered, "Are there not twelve hours of daylight? Those who walk during the day do not stumble, because they see the light of this world"' (Jn 11.9). Jesus' presence as light enables sight and protects us from the darkness that threatens to conquer light, but which ultimately has no power over it. This allows us to become children of light: 'While you have the light, believe in the light, so that you may become children of light' (Jn 12.36).

This light of Jesus does not displace the light of the God of Israel. But the God who hides himself (Isa. 45.15) is now fully present in the light who is Jesus. At the Transfiguration (Mk 9.2–8) we behold the glory of God, again, on a mountaintop. This time the light of Jesus is not like the flames of the burning bush at the giving of the Divine Name (Exod. 3). His light is not like God's glory passing by Moses protected in the cleft of the rock (Exod. 33). It is not like the light on Moses' veiled face at the second giving of the Law (Exod. 34.29–35; cf. 2 Cor. 3.13–16). At the Transfiguration the glory of God is on the very person of the Word incarnate, Israel's Law dramatically present in human flesh.

And what is the response of Peter, James and John, who are privileged to be present with Jesus at his Transfiguration? They are overwhelmed at the vision of his glory. Addressing him with the Hebrew word for teacher, *rabbi*, they are ready to tame the burst of light at Jesus' glory. Peter suggests building three booths (NRSV: 'dwellings' [Gk: *skene*; Heb: *sukkoth*]). This may be a reference to the booths of the feast of Sukkoth, which commemorates the Israelites' wandering in the wilderness. Here Peter, James and John seemingly want to honour Jesus by building a booth for him in addition to the ones for Moses (the Lawgiver) and Elijah (Prophet and forerunner of the Messiah). For Peter, Jesus would then have his place among the 'greats' of the Hebrew religious leaders. But Jesus already has that – he is greater than they. Peter seems not to have realized this.

The Jewish festival of *Sukkoth* itself is now associated with the closing of the cycle of reading of the Law, the Torah, the first five books of the Bible. The cycle is then re-opened at the end of the festival, at *Simchat Torah*, and the readings start again with Genesis 1. The festival is accompanied by great joy and dancing around the Torah scrolls. While we do not know, of course, if these particular traditions existed in Jesus' time, the festival of Sukkoth and the practice of building booths certainly did (Lev. 23).

Jesus himself is the embodiment of the joy of that festival. He is the Word of the Torah scrolls. Peter gets at least one thing right: the glory of the LORD who accompanied Israel during their desert wanderings to freedom rests on this man whose name means 'One who Saves'. The glory that Peter, James and John see on the face of Jesus is the light that was within the burning bush, the light that was in the fiery pillar accompanying Israel on their journey and the light that shines outward within our darkness.

The light at the incarnation of Christ is linked with the Father in our liturgy. The *Phos Hilaron* at Evening Prayer is a song of praise to the Light, which is identified with Jesus the Son:

> O gracious Light, pure brightness of the everliving Father in heaven, O Jesus Christ, holy and blessed!
>
> Now as we come to the setting of the sun, and our eyes behold the vesper light, we sing thy praises, O God: Father, Son, and Holy Spirit.
>
> Thou art worthy at all times to be praised by happy voices, O Son of God, O Giver of life, and to be glorified through all the worlds. (BCP, p. 64)

Most of us today, unlike in the earliest Church, are Gentiles. As such, we are by all rights outsiders to the house of Israel. But now we reach for the hem of Jesus' robe, a fulfilment of Zechariah's prophecy that Gentiles from every nation and tongue and tribe will grab the robe of a Jew, as we search for God: 'Thus says the LORD of hosts: "In those days ten men from nations of every language shall take hold of a Jew, grasping his garment and saying, 'Let us go with you, for we have heard that God is with you'"' (Zech. 8.23). Those of us who are Gentile Christians are that *minyan* who seek to be saved by the fringes of Jesus' prayer shawl. Israel itself is a type of Christ, and the type does not simply disappear at the arrival of its antitype.[10]

This is the God who promises His presence with Israel in an unbreakable covenant. But the fact that the Church identifies Jesus with Israel's God was and continues to be an offence to those who worship the Name of YHWH in Exodus 3.15 alone, no less now than in Jesus' day:

> This was why the Jews sought all the more to kill him, because he not only broke the sabbath but also called God his Father, making himself equal with God. (Jn 5.18)

This offence, however, nullifies neither the truth of God's unity in three persons, nor the permanence of God's covenant with Israel. God does not lie.

The 'Christ hymn' of Philippians 2 that we read on Palm Sunday seems to incorporate a tradition that Paul has already received before writing. This is not the first time that an earlier tradition is quoted or referred to in the New Testament, to be sure. But here in the Christ hymn we find a brief meditation in poetic form that sums up Christian confession of the Divine Name in Jesus. The hymn seems to come in two parts, the first about Jesus' humanity, crucifixion and death:

Let the same mind be in you that was in Christ Jesus, who, though he was in the form of God, did not regard equality with God as something to be exploited, but emptied himself, taking the form of a slave, being born in human likeness. And being found in human form, he humbled himself and became obedient to the point of death – even death on a cross. (Phil. 2.5–8)

The second part is linked to it with the word 'therefore', and tells how God exalted Jesus and bestowed upon him the Name above every Name:

Therefore God also highly exalted him and gave him the name that is above every name, so that at the name of Jesus every knee should bend, in heaven and on earth and under the earth, and every tongue should confess that Jesus Christ is Lord, to the glory of God the Father. (Phil. 2.9–11)

There are a number of things apparent about the name of Jesus here. First, the name of Jesus is associated with his humanity and his willingness to die on the cross. Second, the name of Jesus accompanies his being exalted after being humbled. Third, the name is a gift of the Father. Fourth, the name of Jesus is above every name. Fifth, the name of Jesus commands our worship and confession of that name itself. Sixth, the ultimate goal of the Father's gift of the name of Jesus is our worship of the Father.

This recalls the goal of God's liberating Israel from bondage in Egypt: to worship the Name. The name of Jesus is not a static gift, but is a drawing of all creation toward the glory of God the Father.

Jesus and the LORD

But does the name of Jesus eclipse the Divine Name revealed in Exodus 3.15? Of course not. How could it? God the Holy Trinity is undivided. However the name the Church worships is indeed pronounceable, unlike the Divine Name of Exodus 3, YHWH. Christians are not tied to the same constrictions with regard to the Name of God, as devout Jews understand their texts to demand of them. Jesus has a face that we can indeed behold through the witness of the disciples and the early church, in the power of the Holy Spirit, in Scripture, in our worship and in each other. From now on the Name that demands our worship is the name of Jesus. We are invited to use the name of Jesus. We are privileged to address the Father through him. The name of Jesus is itself the presence of God.

Long ago God spoke to our ancestors in many and various ways by the prophets, but in these last days he has spoken to us by a Son, whom he appointed heir of all things, through whom he also created the worlds. He is the reflection of God's glory and the exact imprint of God's very being, and he sustains all things by his powerful word. When he had made purification for sins, he sat down at the right hand of the Majesty on high, having become as much superior to angels as the name he has inherited is more excellent than theirs. (Heb. 1.1–3)

But the name Jesus inherited does not eclipse the unpronounceable name, YHWH. Jesus is the Word of God spoken through the prophets (Heb. 1.1). God now speaks through him, the divinely appointed heir (Heb. 1.2). Jesus is the reflection of God's glory and the imprint of God's being who purified us (Heb. 1.3). God entrusted Jesus with His own power when He raised him from the dead and seated him at his right hand far above all authority and dominion. Indeed, God gives Jesus his own name for the protection of the flock (Jn 17.11). But God is not two-faced.

The name of Jesus is above every name that is named, not only in this age, but also in the age to come. God has put all things under Jesus' feet and has made him the head over all things for the Church, which is his body, the fullness of him who fills all in all. And all who worship the Name of Jesus are that body (Eph. 1.21–23). But the God of Israel does not thereby cease to exist. The promises of the God of Israel are everlasting. The antitype does not obliterate its type. Christians know those promises to be bound to the life, death and resurrection of the Son. This is what it means to read typologically: the fundamental link is sacramental.

Honouring the Name of Jesus may be very difficult for us. Because we do not share the Jewish tradition of protecting the Divine Name in written or spoken usage, holding the Name in highest respect may not come easily for us. The name 'Jesus' is certainly pronounceable, and we have indeed been invited to use it in prayer and supplication. But because the name Jesus itself participates in the reality of the Divine Name revealed in Exodus 3.15, it is by extension included in the commandment against using the name of God in vain: 'You shall not make wrongful use of the name of the LORD your God, for the LORD will not acquit anyone who misuses his name' (Exod. 20.7).

The practical implications for our daily lives are deep and broad. Some of us may live in cultures where the very use of the name Jesus in worship can result in loss of life and limb. Others may live in contexts where the name Jesus is used for many purposes other than worship, from common complaint to exclamation of surprise to expression of frustration and anger. We may become inured by such uses of the Name. For us Christians it can become a challenge to observe the commandment regarding the respect and protection of the divine name.

When one uses the name regularly enough in adoration, and worship, however, hearing it used in a disrespectful way can seem jarring. Just imagine how strange it would be if someone were to curse or damn using the name of his or her spouse. It would certainly indicate something amiss in that relationship. 'So the tongue is a little member and boasts of great things. How great a forest is set ablaze by a small fire!' (Jas 3.5). Nevertheless, the casual disrespect for the name soaks into our bones.

Occasionally, I find myself in conversation with someone who uses the name as curse or exclamation in my presence. People who know that I am a priest will sometimes offer me an awkward apology. They are embarrassed that they may have offended me. I tell them that I just thought they were praying. That often elicits silence. It is certainly one way to discourage people from misusing the name of Jesus in my presence.

The Divine Name and Purifying Fire

In *My Bright Abyss* Christian Wiman says the love of God is 'like a simple kiss that has a bite of starlight to it'.[11] This is beautiful, but too easy, too smooth, too comfortable. It does not capture the fuller sense of the Bible's rendering of God's love in the name of Jesus. In Scripture we find that God both kisses and bites and while the kiss of God is sweet, the bite of God can sting. But we can't have the starlight of God's presence without both His sweet kiss and His stinging bite. The kiss of God is the Incarnation, patterned forth in the covenant with Abraham and his descendants. The stinging bite is Jesus' abandonment on the cross patterned in Israel's exile from the holy city of Jerusalem.

We find both God's sweet kiss and stinging bite in Malachi 3. There, we hear that priests will be prepared for the Day of the LORD, and that this will require their purification. The prophet declares that the LORD will purify and prepare His priests for the Day of the LORD, when God will be finally and fully present. But passing through fire does not promise to be a comfortable experience.

> See, I am sending my messenger to prepare the way before me, and the Lord whom you seek will suddenly come to his temple. The messenger of the covenant in whom you delight – indeed, he is coming, says the LORD of hosts. But who can endure the day of his coming, and who can stand when he appears? For he is like a refiner's fire and like fullers' soap; he will sit as a refiner and purifier of silver, and he will purify the descendants of Levi and refine them like gold and silver, until they present offerings to the LORD in righteousness. Then the offering of Judah and Jerusalem will be pleasing to the LORD as in the days of old and as in former years. (Mal. 3.1–4)

The libretto of Handel's glorious oratorio *Messiah* is stitched together from Scripture. The famous chorus, 'And He Shall Purify', sings of the fiery and purifying presence as an integral episode in the story of the Gospel. When we come to the point in the score where the choir sings the words 'And He Shall Purify ...' we can almost hear Handel paint in vivid colours the licking flames that will purify the sons of Levi. But why does God need these flames? No one likes fire. It hurts. But it purifies us for proper worship of the God who is present among us.

As the final book of the Old Testament, Malachi points us toward the coming 'messenger of the covenant' (Mal. 3.1).[12] God will purify the sons of Levi, the tribe of priests from whom Moses is descended. Only thus will they be able to offer to the LORD the sacrifice of righteousness. And this is the purpose for which they had originally been ordained. Jesus Christ is that pure and righteous sacrifice for the World. He is both the One who sacrifices and the sacrifice itself. He is both 'priest and sacrifice'. But it is not only of Levites or of ordained clergy that we Christians need to think of here. This fire licks at the priesthood of all believers. This purifying fire itself is indeed a kiss that transforms us to a place beyond starlight. But it does not allow us to escape God's bite.

Jesus' sacrifice and our praise are linked. We offer in our own lives before God the sacrifice of ourselves. At the consecration, one of the Eucharistic prayers expresses this element with the

words: 'accept this our sacrifice of praise and thanksgiving ...'
(BCP, p. 335). Our praises and thanksgivings do more than just
cheer our hearts. They enthrone God: 'Yet you are the Holy One,
enthroned upon the praises of Israel ...' (Ps. 22.3). These words
are from the same psalm that Jesus quotes from the cross: 'My
God, my God, why have you abandoned me?' (22.1). Jesus the
Righteous One of Israel is now purified in the burning fire and
sacrifice of forsakenness. Enthroning God in praise, he himself
is crowned in abandonment.

The image of God's enthronement on the praises of Israel
points us to the visions in the Revelation to John. The One
enthroned (Rev. 4.2) is met by flashes of lightning and peals of
thunder (Rev. 4.5). The four living creatures and the twenty-four
elders respond in praise (Rev. 4.6–11). All of these people, who
are not limited to Israel but include them, sing praises (Rev. 7.5).
In a mixing of metaphors and twisting of imagery the scene is
almost unimaginable. The Lamb who is also Shepherd sits on
the throne. He is declared to be the one who 'will guide [us] to
springs of the water of life, and [...] will wipe away every tear
from [our] eyes' (Rev. 7.17).

God proves and tests the people in the light of His fire for the
sake of His glory, not to give us wisdom or pleasure or even to
teach us a lesson. God's purifying of us is not for God's pleasure
either, as though God were some sado-masochistic tyrant. God's
purifying is however for God's own glory.

For my name's sake I defer my anger, for the sake of my praise I restrain it for you, so that I may not cut you off. See, I have refined you, but not like silver; I have tested you in the furnace of adversity. For my own sake, for my own sake, I do it, for why should my name be profaned? My glory I will not give to another. (Isa. 48.9–11)

Why should God's name be profaned, indeed? It is through this name that we know God and worship Him. In this we find the Father's sacrifice of even His own Name and identity, demanding our worship and praise.

What this means for Christians as we behold the cross is striking. It is there that God empties Himself, divesting Himself even of His own identity and presence. 'My God, my God, why have you abandoned me?' (Ps. 22.1). Jesus' agony on the cross in his Cry of Dereliction in Psalm 22 is gathered up into the context of the whole psalm. His cry bleeds all the way down to verse 11: 'Be not far from me, for trouble is near, and there is none to help' (22.11). Jesus calls on God's presence even at his moment of abandonment: he knows that God is indeed not present. Yet he also knows that God is the only one whose true presence he most needs.

Even in his own awareness of being abandoned by God, Jesus does not curse the Name. We will later find Job's response to his own suffering fits this pattern and as such witnesses to Christ. Job, like Jesus, does not curse God. Yet Job, unlike Jesus, cannot do for us what only Jesus can do. Jesus endures God's very abandonment that will be overturned only on the other side of death. But Jesus' abandonment is not erased. He is truly forsaken in our stead. After the resurrection when Jesus meets us, we will know God to be the One who will never again abandon us. He is King, enthroned upon the praises of Israel and on the hymns of the Church. And in his Name is our true worship and praise, transforming and purifying us. Even when seemingly distant, when none seems present to help, Jesus is nevertheless with us and will not forsake: 'I am with you always . . .' (Mt 28.20).

> At the Name of Jesus, every knee shall bow,
> Every tongue confess Him King of glory now;
> 'Tis the Father's pleasure we should call Him Lord,
> Who from the beginning was the mighty Word.
>
> Caroline M. Noel (1870)

The Divine Name in the Incarnation: I AM

At the end of the Gospel according to Matthew Jesus describes his identity by using a phrase similar to the one we heard in Exodus 3.14. There, we saw that in advance of the revelation of the name itself, its interpretation is given: 'I AM WHO I AM.' In the pre-Christian Greek translation of the Hebrew Bible known as the Septuagint, Exodus 3.14 gives us *ego eimi ho on* for 'I AM WHO I AM. These words are very close to the Greek words we hear on Jesus' lips in his *I am* statements in the gospels.

Jesus' 'I am' (*ego eimi*) statements can be heard as allusions to the 'I am' of Exodus 3.14. These self-designations indicate Jesus' identification with the God who revealed His name to Moses, YHWH. We hear in Jesus' *I am* statements that he is life itself: its source, sustenance and goal. Jesus is protector of our lives, even to the point of giving over his own life: '*I am* the gate for the sheep ... *I am* the Good Shepherd. The Good Shepherd lays down his life for the sheep' (Jn 10.7–11). When Jesus speaks of his disciples' following him, he tells us that we are to be where he is: 'Whoever serves me must follow me, and where *I am*, there will my servant be also. Whoever serves me, the Father will honour' (Jn 12.26). Being in Jesus' presence is linked to loving and honouring the Father. It is also linked to new life. At the raising of Lazarus Jesus says '*I am* the resurrection and the life' (Jn 11.25).

Jesus also tells us that he is life-sustainer: '*I am* the bread of life. Whoever comes to me will never be hungry, and whoever believes in me will never be thirsty' (Jn 6.35). He is the path

to the Father: '*I am* the way, and the truth, and the life. No
one comes to the Father except through me' (Jn 14.6). Jesus
is our organic link and access both to the Father and to each
other: '*I am* the true vine, and my Father is the vinegrower
... *I am* the vine, you are the branches. Those who abide in
me and I in them bear much fruit, because apart from me you
can do nothing' (Jn 15.1, 5). Being in relation to Jesus in this
way means that we are specifically also related to each other. In
this, being in relation to Jesus is also tied to bearing the fruit
of good works. This means that being in his presence is not a
static state. It is tied to our ethical life. It is bound closely to
our sanctification. Being exposed in, to, and by his light, we
are transformed.

These good works manifest themselves in service: 'For who is
greater, the one who is at the table or the one who serves? Is it not
the one at the table? But *I am* among you as one who serves' (Lk.
22.27). And we have his ultimate presence as we ourselves carry
forth his earthly ministry. Jesus remains with us as we teach and
baptize in his name: '*I am* with you always, to the end of the age'
(Mt. 28.20).

One of the most important of these 'I am' statements is in
the Gospel according to Mark, the earliest among the Christian
gospels. Shortly after his betrayal by Judas and his subsequent
arrest, Jesus is brought before the Council. They are looking for
charges that would merit the death penalty, but the witnesses'

testimonies are contradictory. Finally, after Jesus is silent among his accusers on the several unproven charges, the high priest asks Jesus point-blank 'Are you the Messiah, the Son of the Blessed One? (Mk 14.61). Jesus' response is to acknowledge this charge by saying simply '*I am*; and you will see the Son of man seated at the right hand of Power, and coming with the clouds of heaven' (Mk 14.62).

But this linking of past, present and future in the person of Jesus is not unique to his interview before the High Priest. Jesus' words here are profoundly evocative of his relationship to the God of Israel. He openly admits that his identity is tied to the One whose Name was revealed to Moses in Exodus 3.15. His own presence among them not only fits the past revelation, but also the future Coming One and the end of time when God's presence will be everlasting. In the words of the Nicene Creed, 'His Kingdom will have no end.'

Jesus is the beginning and the end, the Alpha and the Omega: '"*I am* the Alpha and the Omega," says the Lord God, who is and who was and who is to come, the Almighty' (Rev. 1.8). The remarkable thing in these two verses is the ordering and tenses of the verb 'to be'. While we might have expected Jesus to be the one who *was* and *is* and *is to come*, as though in chronological order that is not what we hear at this point from him. The present tense comes first, not in the middle between past and future, which might make more intuitive sense. This means that the primary mode of Jesus' being among us is in the present tense. He is presence, in the present, in the present tense.

Indeed, the present is the only moment that truly exists in all of human life, whether we honour God or not. Regret dwells in the past, and anxiety sits uneasily in the future. We are told that, for our mental health, we must 'live in the moment'. The present is the only moment we truly have. And Jesus, even in his present is-ness, is inseparable from the merciful deeds of God in the past. He is also tied firmly to God's promised future.

Jesus is the present tense, the one who is ('I AM WHO I AM', Exod. 3.14). Jesus is the past tense, the one who was ('In the beginning God created ...' [Gen. 1.1]; 'In the beginning was the word ...' [Jn 1.1]). And Jesus is the future tense, the one who is to come ('When you pass through the waters, I will be with you' [Isa. 43.2]; 'I am with you always to the end ...' [Mt. 28.20]). Being in the presence of Jesus in our worship is all of these moments together at once: past, present and future.

Being in Jesus' presence is more than the 'being in the moment' of mindfulness meditation. It is indeed somewhat like that. But Jesus' presence is itself eternity. Being in his presence brings us eternal life. And this is why we can taste hints of eternity even in the present tense of our earthly lives, when we come into the presence of Jesus in Word and Sacrament. 'Even so, come, Lord Jesus.'

Questions for further reflection

- If Jesus were to give one of his 'I AM' statements to you, what would it be? Would it be one he has already given in Scripture, or a new one?
- How do you understand the cry of dereliction (Ps. 22.1)? Was Jesus truly abandoned on the cross?
- What does your answer to the above question say about Good Friday, Holy Saturday, and Easter?
- If Jesus were to purify the Church today, what would be burnt up, and what would be left over? What would we become?

5

First Watch: God's Questions, Our Answers

Elijah

There are times in our lives when all is dark and we fail to see even a glimmer of light. In our darkest places, we ask seemingly unanswerable questions. Even in the simplest Bible stories, where we might not immediately recognize suffering, people cry out to God in complaint and question. In these stories, we hear questions from people to God, from God to people, and back again. These questions test the identities of the ones who ask, and prove the identity of the One who responds. But the roles are often reversed: sometimes it is God who asks, and it is the people who must respond.

In the story of Elijah at Horeb in 1 Kings 19, we find this sort of a dialogue. Elijah's actions elicit God's questions. Elijah is hiding in the cave there on the mountain. We remember that Horeb is the same mountain where the Divine Name was revealed in Exodus 3 and where the Law was given in chapter 20 (cf. Exod. 34; Deut. 5). Elijah has just participated in the LORD's triumph over Baal in the miraculous fire at Mount Carmel (1 Kgs 18.20–40). Now he is hiding from Queen Jezebel's murderous servants. She has put a price on Elijah's life for his prophecies against her and King Ahab: they have worshipped Baal and Asherah instead of the LORD. Even so, after this persecution on behalf of God, 'The hand of the LORD was on Elijah' (18.46).

By this point, Elijah finds his life too heavy a burden to bear, and asks the LORD to take it away. Elijah seeks release from his persecutors, who want to murder him because of his words against Jezebel and Ahab. He lies down under a broom tree, seeking simply to die a peaceful death (1 Kgs 19:9). But the LORD will not allow him this easy way out. The LORD will not leave Elijah alone.

Instead, the LORD provides sustenance – food through the ministry of an angel. The food is not just for the relief of hunger, or for Elijah's pleasure. The text makes it clear that the food is to keep him strong for the road ahead: 'Get up and eat, otherwise the journey will be too much for you' (19.7). The LORD still has work for Elijah.

Later, the word of the LORD – apparently an agent in its own right – comes to Elijah and tells him to leave the cave (19.12ff.). Then Elijah experiences terrifying signs: wind, earthquake and fire. The LORD's presence is not to be found in any of these. Then a silence descends: not an absence, but a terrifying alien presence. Elijah encounters this alien presence in a sound of sheer silence.[13] While the text does not say specifically that God is present in the silence, it omits what had been said after each of the other experiences: in all three, wind, earthquake and fire, the LORD was specifically not present.

But even in this silence, there is a voice, and we hear the same question God asked of Elijah earlier as he was hiding in the cave (1 Kgs 19.9): 'What are you doing here, Elijah?' God does not give up on Elijah but insists that he serve Him. This voice commands Elijah to get off his hind quarters and come out of hiding. He is to act even in spite of his fears. He is to return to Damascus and anoint kings and a prophet who will succeed him. Even in Elijah's despair and fear that he is the only one left faithful to the God of Israel, God tells him that there are still thousands who are like him. There will in fact be a future, and God has called Elijah to help usher it in.

And so Elijah is a figure of hope for the future reign of God. The prophet Malachi (4.5) identifies Elijah as the one who will be sent 'before the great and terrible day of the LORD comes'. And so at the Passover meal, the Jewish custom is to leave a chair empty and a place set for Elijah, and to keep the door to the house slightly ajar, in case he should come and usher in the end time. The gospels identify John the Baptist as Elijah come again, the forerunner of the Messiah Jesus and the herald of the end time.

Job's Questions, God's Questions

As we saw with Elijah's hiding in the cave, so now we find God responding to Job's complaints with further questions. Near the conclusion of the book, we read that God answers Job out of the whirlwind. God reveals Himself not by giving His name or identity, nor by speaking about Himself, but by asking about Job.

> Who is this that darkens counsel by words without knowledge? Gird up your loins like a man, I will question you, and you shall declare to me. (Job 38.2–3)

God's response is not very satisfying, to say the least. It too is a series of questions. Even in God's 'answer' there is no comforting word to Job, no hint that everything will be fine in the end. God does not come out from hiding, does not unveil his unknowability, does not give Job a clue as to His inscrutable ways. It is only in that very hiddenness and within this unknowability that Job meets God. God reveals Himself to Job only as a stranger, the One who faces Job, the One to whom Job in his terror and agony cries out.

God does not re-introduce Himself, or say 'I am the Creator of the foundations of the earth …' God simply asks a question which demands Job's response: 'Where were you when I laid the foundation of the earth: tell me if you have any understanding …' (38.4).God tells Job who He is only by noting Job's complete ignorance of the divine identity. God puts Job in his place. Yet even in this place, Job is within the embrace of God. Even in this place of complete instability ('where were you …?') is mercy, justice, grace. It is a place of mercy because it is a place where God dwells, even though as accuser and questioner.

This is God's response to Job out of the whirlwind, a response that is a question: who are you in relation to me? The implied answer God would have Job give is: I am yours. And God would agree: You are not your own. You are mine.

And so Paul will say to the church at Corinth 'you are not your own. You were bought with a price, therefore glorify God in your body' (1 Cor. 6.19–20). Even in that body which I have broken, even in that life which I have shattered, you are mine. Whether you like it or not, I am with you.

Memory and Hope

As with God's response to Job, so with us: sometimes God's answers to our desperate cries come as a reminder about God's identity, about who God is. The Baal Shem Tov, the eighteenth-century mystic and founder of Hasidic Jewish piety, once said that exile comes from forgetting and redemption comes with memory. Exile comes upon Israel when they forget God and turn away from God's Law. Like Adam and Eve expelled from the presence of God in the Garden of Eden, Israel is sent far from God's presence when they forget their sacred bond.

For us, too, forgetting leads to our own exile. And returning to the presence of God means returning to the table where Christ is present. In the Eucharistic liturgy, we too recall the saving acts of God: 'we remember [Christ's] death, we proclaim his resurrection, we await his coming in glory' (BCP, p. 368). When we, for whatever reason, cease to enter into that memory, we all too easily lose sight of our communal redemption. We as·a people wander in the wilderness, in a world where violence seems to reign. We wander in exile from God and even from ourselves. We forget to give thanks for God's blessings and graciousness, because we prefer to see these things as though they were mere coincidences. Gifts call for thankfulness. Coincidences can be ignored.

And yet even in the wilderness where we seem to forget God, memory that points to the future is what sustains us. There is a story of a rabbi in one of the concentration camps of Nazi Germany. He knew that his people were suffering gravely and had lost hope. The people gathered around him and said 'Rabbi, God does not hear our prayers. God has abandoned us in our sufferings. The God of our people does indeed sleep. (Ps 121:4) The LORD of Israel does not hear us.' The rabbi responded: 'What then shall we do?' They did what they knew to do: they prayed the *Shema* as they always had first thing in the morning and last thing at night. This reminded them of who God is and who they are in relation to that God: '*Hear, O Israel, the LORD your God, the LORD alone. You shall love the LORD your God with all your heart, and with all your soul, and with all your might*' (Deut. 6.4–5). They belonged to the LORD, and all they knew to do was to pray in the words that LORD had given them.[14]

Even in their sufferings, when all has seemed lost, even in their exile and in the annihilation of so many, Israel finds itself, as always, face to face with God. Whether they like it or not, as Erasmus said, God was with them. As Job consistently clung to God even in his complaints, so too did this rabbi and his people. God continues to be present, all appearances to the contrary.

So when things seem entirely lost, and we give up on God, what do we do? Hopefully, and by the grace of God, we will remind ourselves that despite all appearances, God Is. God is with us. God is for us. We will help each other remember the identity of God: I AM WHO I AM. The people of God is not just a collection of individuals, but a web of relationships created by God. We are not our own. We are not on our own.

Sometimes our living through pain is a sheer hanging on to the very tips of the fringes of Jesus' prayer shawl. In the previous chapter, we noted how through the prophet Zechariah God tells the people that he will bring them back to Jerusalem from exile and will dwell again with them there (Zech. 8.1–7). This will be such a remarkable time that ten men even from all the nations of the earth will say: 'Let us go with you, for we hear that God is with you' (Zech. 8.23). Ten Jewish men make up a *minyan*, the minimum necessary for corporate Jewish daily prayer. But the prophet seems to speak here of a Gentile *minyan*. It makes no sense; it is a category mistake. But God's future will be just that remarkable. Who is this Jew whose prayer shawl will be a magnet for the Gentiles? Jesus of Nazareth, Emmanuel, God-with-us. The fringes of this Jew's prayer shawl are a sign of the future promise, the hope of redemption, the restoration beyond exile, the resurrection of the dead.

Jesus: Our Hope Beyond Exile

This Jew, Jesus, draws Gentiles into the people of Israel. And yet Gentiles occupy a place that is potentially 'unclean'. However, being 'clean or unclean' is not a distinction of the Gentile religious world. This concept is certainly one that is not easily grasped in the Church, much less in the secular world. There are stories in the Gospels, however, where Jesus physically touches an unclean person, healing him or her. We don't fully grasp the sheer audacity of such an act unless we have a sense of what it means to be unclean according to the Law. God's presence in the Law defines what makes for pure and impure. It is the presence of God in Jesus Christ that allows him to purify even the impure, to cleanse even the unclean.

We find in the Law that lepers are among the unclean. They were to be avoided at all costs so that their impurity, as though a religious contagion, would not be 'passed along'. They were in exile in their own homes. Dead bodies and graves were also unclean. The story in John 11 of the raising of Lazarus should strike us afresh when we remember this. Grotesque things like bodily discharges also made a person ritually unclean. But being ritually unclean did not mean that the body itself is somehow evil. For the Hebrew faith, the body is good. And we find this to be the case when Jesus heals people by touching them with his own body or even simply his clothing. (See also Mark 6.56).

In Luke 8.43–48, Jesus heals a woman who has a haemorrhagic disease. The text does not tell us what this malady is; we can only guess. Whatever it was, it has made her ritually unclean because it involved spilling of blood. She asks an implicit question in her action, and makes an implicit demand of Jesus. In silence she approaches him, asking without words to be healed. As a righteous

Jew in obedience to the Law (Lev. 15.25–27), Jesus should avoid her uncleanness. Certainly he would know this. She, too, should know better, because apparently she herself is a Jew. Nevertheless, she dares to approach Jesus. She dares to demand healing from this one who she knows can heal. She reaches out and touches the fringes of his prayer shawl. The story tells us that Jesus knows she has touched him: he himself asks a question 'Who touched me?' (Lk. 8.45) In the woman's fear, she does not answer.

But her act shows that she understands who he is, and who she is before him. The impurity of her flow of blood is cleansed by the flow of healing from Jesus through her touch of even just his clothing. She knows that, as Zechariah 8 had prophesied, God is present in this man who is the sign of the fulfilment of the promises to Israel. She reaches out for him in a silent plea. Jesus takes upon himself her uncleanness, cleansing her.

Like this woman in Luke 8 who is unclean, we each approach Jesus and reach out to him. We have heard that he is the very presence of God, and so we ask for his healing touch. In worship we come to the altar where he is truly present. We touch his body, we receive it in our hands and take it into our own bodies. We drink his blood. Our impurity is taken up into his purity and we are made clean. But he himself is not made impure by our impurity. In the presence of Jesus, we are not the infectious diseases we might think ourselves to be. But we have to approach him. We must ask, even if wordlessly. And if we listen, we hear him ask us: 'Who touched me?' Then we will know we are clean. Then we can give thanks, as did the woman who reached out to him, was made clean, and fell at Jesus' feet.

The Suffering Servant

The Suffering Servant of Isaiah 53 points graphically to the sufferings of Christ. As with the Suffering Servant, so with Christ: there is no reason that we should want to look upon Jesus at his crucifixion. On the cross he had no beauty that we should want to embrace him. And yet it was God's will that he should suffer. Reflecting on Jesus' crucifixion is not often an uplifting experience for us. And yet, says Isaiah,

> [H]e hath no form nor comeliness; and when we shall see him, there is no beauty that we should desire him. He is despised and rejected of men; a man of sorrows, and acquainted with grief: and we hid as it were our faces from him; he was despised, and we esteemed him not. Surely he hath borne our griefs, and carried our sorrows: yet we did esteem him stricken, smitten of God, and afflicted. But he was wounded for our transgressions, he was bruised for our iniquities: the chastisement of our peace was upon him; and with his stripes we are healed. (Isa. 53.2–5; KJV)

It is Jesus' wounds that bind our own. This man Jesus whom we see patterned forth in Isaiah's Suffering Servant is the antitype to the type in Isaiah 53, embraces our sorrows and hands them back to us soaked in his own blood, the blood that heals. This means that no pain is merely random for those who pick up the cross. Our pain has a purpose, but it is a purpose we can only begin to discern from within Jesus' own wounds, on the other side of the resurrection. Our pain is enclosed in Christ's love and mercy and healing. If by the power of the Holy Spirit we can bear our pain, it can sow in us new life.

We know this is the case because even in Jesus' risen life he still bears the scars of his crucifixion. It is in fact those very scars that bear his identity as risen Lord to his disciples. Jesus proves that he is no ghost but truly himself by showing the disciples his wounds (Lk. 24.39–40). Only by seeing the marks of the nails in Jesus' hands, feet and side does Thomas realize who Jesus is, and only then does he confess him as Lord and God (Jn 20.26–28).

Some of the biblical prophets bear the vocation of voicing the people's pain. Jeremiah laments Israel's exile from the land, the land where God had promised to be present to His people. The prophet cries out on behalf of the covenant people who have been repeatedly unfaithful to God, and questions God.

Why is my pain unceasing, my wound incurable, refusing to be healed? Truly, you are to me like a deceitful brook,

> like waters that fail ... For thus says the LORD: Your hurt is
> incurable, your wound is grievous. (Jer. 15.18; 30.12)

Instead of healing, this God assails. Jeremiah takes on the role of
the people even in this, even in their agony. Jesus will later also
take on the role of the people Israel in their desolation.

Examples abound throughout the prophets. Micah likewise
cries out in agony at the punishment of the LORD, which inflicts
a wound that cannot be healed: 'For her wound is incurable. It has
come to Judah; it has reached to the gate of my people, to Jerusalem'
(Mic. 1.9). But why this wound? Why this suffering? Should not a
good God keep such pain from His beloved? Our pain is, however,
not random. God purposefully casts Israel out from the land, the
covenant gift where God dwells. In their disobedience they cannot
dwell in God's presence without being annihilated. Their exile is
in fact God's mercy. While this merciful and loving God seems to
have revoked his promises to his people. God is not untrue to His
own word. God has not abandoned His people, His people have
abandoned their God. It is only Jesus who will be truly abandoned,
so that the people will never again pass through such an experience.

Mary's Wounds

One of the most striking things about Christian Scripture is that,
while we find prophecy and fulfilment within the Old Testament,

and from the Old Testament to the New Testament, we also find this patterning forth of the cross and resurrection within the New Testament itself. We find the cross and resurrection foreshadowed long before the events surrounding Jesus' adult life. The fact that even Mary will experience the cross as suffering is made clear to the reader long in advance of the Passion, indeed even at Jesus' infancy.

In Luke 2 when Mary and Joseph bring Jesus to the Temple for his Presentation according to the Law of Moses, Even while Simeon prophecies the joy and hope that this infant will bring to the covenant people, he also declares that the baby will bring light to those outside of the covenant as well. Jesus will be 'a light for revelation to the Gentiles and for the glory of [God's] people Israel' (Lk. 2.31–32). Simeon then turns to Mary with another prophecy: 'a sword will pierce your own soul, too' (Lk. 2.35). Mary's fate is sealed with her son's. His cross will shatter her along with him, and it will heal her, too, along with the rest of the world.

The pilgrimage route of Santiago de Compostela was one of the three most significant pilgrimage routes of medieval Christian piety. Today it still exists as a web of journeys leading across Europe. There are many points of origin, but one goal: the shrine of St James the Apostle in northern Spain. In the villages along the Way of St James, there stand at many of the village squares large stone crucifixes where pilgrims can pray and mark yet another stage on their journey. Especially in the province of Galicia, where Santiago lies, these crucifixes are unique. Made of stone and standing some five meters high, they hold Jesus at his death on one face, and Mary in her own agony on the opposite face. He is nailed to one side, dying; she stands on the other side, weeping. On some of these crucifixes, an iron sword pierces the stone of Mary's breast. Jesus' suffering is her own. A sword pierces her own soul, as in the prophecy of the old man Simeon.

This is true to a certain extent of the pain any mother would feel in Mary's position. We mothers are each so intimately bound to the well-being of our child that anything our child suffers, so we likewise suffer. A good mother would rather take on the suffering of her child than witness her child's pain. But we are not Mary, and our children are not Jesus. For this crucifix, for this mother, for this son, there is a deeper message.

In the fifth century, Mary's identity is finally given a term that sums up what Christians had been trying to say about her all along: she is *theotokos*, God-bearer. As mother of Jesus, she bears the Son of God to the world. As such, she indicates to each of us our common vocation: to bear Jesus into the world. To nurture Jesus. To show him to others, the way a mother proudly shows off her child.

Jesus is a living person. He is not just a symbol of a generic human reality separable from his own specific identity. Mary is one of the only two personal locators in the creeds who pinpoint Jesus' non-mythic presence. The other such person is Pontius Pilate. Mary bears the Christ: Pilate murders him. We each are meant to be God-bearers, but despite our own best intentions we often participate in Pilate's role as Christ's murderers. It is our most joyful blessing to bear Christ. It is our deepest sorrow to slay him. Yet even there Christ is present in healing.

What is healing, then? In my own experience it has rarely if ever meant immediate relief from pain. The fourteenth-century English mystic Julian of Norwich assures us 'All shall be well and all shall be well and all manner of thing shall be well.' But this is no smoothing over the rough patches in our lives. Julian is not trying to tell us, in the words of Bobby McFerrin, not to worry but be happy. Julian points to the reality St Paul speaks of in 1 Corinthians: death is the last enemy. Death stings in the present. But death will be swallowed up in victory at the last day (1 Cor. 15.54; cf. Isa. 25.7). All shall be well, says Julian – but not immediately. The future tense points to the end. Here is a call for trust, hope, endurance.

Jesus' Wounds and Ours

The most vivid indicator that the end is still to come is, as we have seen, that Jesus' scars remain even on his resurrected body. Jesus is identifiably present among the disciples after the resurrection in part by the scars he still bears. In his hands and feet and on his side, these wounds identify him to the disciples. The disciples recognize Jesus also in the breaking of the bread, and in his opening to them the scriptures that spoke of his death and resurrection. They know Jesus before his death as teacher and wonder-worker. After his murder and resurrection they know him as Lord of life especially in these wounds that were inflicted as his own earthly life was extinguished.

But these are not two different Jesuses. Even though Jesus has two natures, he has one single identity. He is the same Lord and God whom Peter had confessed at Caesarea. He is the same Lord whose feet Mary had anointed. He is the same Lord whom Judas had betrayed. One of the most profound claims of Christian confession is that Jesus is 'fully human, fully divine'. He is not a little bit divine over here and a little bit human over there. And this is what his wounds show us: even on his resurrected body, his wounds remain. In our own suffering, then, why should we be surprised when our scars remain even after we pray that they be removed? Even after we meet God in Word and Sacrament?

We are indeed called to relieve human suffering wherever we can. Paul commands us to bear one another's burdens and in this way fulfil the law of Christ (Gal. 6.2). But sometimes our relationship to the sufferings of others can be complicated, to our great shame. We like to think of ourselves as wanting to relieve the sufferings of others, and yet we are fascinated by others' pain. Sometimes we look away in horror. Other times we stare as voyeurs. In both, we betray Christ.

The Civil Rights Movement in the United States proved in many ways more painful in the southern states because of the particular history of race relations there. We all know the story: the Revd Dr Martin Luther King, Jr, was engaged in leading a non-violent protest demanding civil rights for Black people in America. Most of these people had ancestors who had been stolen from their homes in West Africa, to be sold as slaves in the Americas and the Caribbean.

In April of 1968, the city of Memphis, Tennessee witnessed a Sanitation Workers' Strike. The striking workers were African American males. They were trying to heed King's pleas to remain non-violent in their protest. So they marched silently. They did not chant slogans, as do many who protest. They wore sandwich boards emblazoned in bold print with simple words: – 'I Am A Man'. The effect was to say 'You should be ashamed of yourselves for looking away from the suffering of another man just like you.' Job said something similar in his own suffering: 'Look at me, and be appalled, and lay your hand upon your mouth' (21.5). Witness my suffering and shut up. These strikers were trying to say that they were not just a class of people. They were individually members of the human species, and of the

American people, with claims to the same civil rights of every other American.

The Revd Dr Martin Luther King, Jr, was visiting Memphis at the time to give support and encouragement to the strikers. He was assassinated there the day after giving his now-famous 'Mountaintop' address. His words in that speech were, of course, a reference to Moses' arriving at the mountaintop. He was permitted only to look out over the land, but not to enter. He never made it. King knew that he himself would not make it to the Promised Land of racial equality in the United States, but he had faith and hope that his people would.

While we have made great strides in the United States since that Sanitation Workers' Strike and King's assassination, King's vision remains elusive. As a country, the United States has not made it to the Promised Land of King's dream. Racial discrimination and violence cause much suffering still, within our governments, our police forces, our education and prison systems, our health care, our industry and commerce. The list goes on. Many miles still lie ahead of us before racial equality is actually won in the USA.

Can we Christians behold the suffering of others as though these others were not one with us? Can we really affirm that all humans are made in the image of God and yet insist on holding those who suffer 'out there', like some sort of contagion? Can we Christians actually avoid the reality that all human suffering is fundamentally participating in the sufferings of Christ? If Christ were to fall before us while carrying his cross, would we not share the role of Simon of Cyrene and bear his cross for him?

We Christians must remind ourselves who we are in the sight of the LORD. We are not a lump of generic humanity thrown into one great melting pot. This is where the mistranslation of the image and likeness of God at Genesis 1.27 becomes tragic. It is not merely a matter of words: we are not 'humanity' until God addresses us. We are not 'humanity' until we are in relation to one another. It is only in our unity in Christ and as we face each other that we are truly one and therefore truly individuals. We are first and foremost the Body of Christ and only then are we individuals: 'You are the body of Christ and individually members of it' (1 Cor. 12.27).

Neither looking away from nor staring at the wounds of others honours the humanity of the sufferer. Jesus always honours the humanity of the other in their own suffering as he takes it up in his own. Yet we would turn away even from him. We find his suffering disgusting and repellent. There is nothing that would attract us to his cross.

> [t]here is no beauty that we should desire him. He is despised and rejected of men; a man of sorrows, and acquainted with grief: and we hid as it were our faces from him; he was despised, and we esteemed him not. (Isa. 53.2–3, KJV)

It is only Jesus' suffering that is redemptive. Other suffering is not. This is part of the reason that Christians are not to seek suffering, as though it were a good in itself. It is only when we bury our own suffering in Jesus' death and wrap his shroud around our pain that human suffering can be redeemed. His cross poses to all of us who gaze on it and who do not turn away questions that confer on us our own identity in him. The responses we hear are not always neat or satisfying. But they are always spoken from within the love and mercy of God. As such, they are grace.

Our Address to God

While we are assured throughout the Bible of God's ultimate presence, the Christian life can mean facing the fact that God's presence sometimes comes in the form of His hiding: 'Truly, you are a God who hides himself', says Isaiah. Notice that this is not a philosophical proposition about God. That might be something more like this: 'The God of Israel is present among us sometimes as hidden.' No – the prophet uses second-person address: '*You are* a God who hides himself.' In the next breath, Isaiah continues his address: 'O God of Israel, the Saviour' (Isa. 45.15). Even as hidden, God's identity remains constant. The same One who has saved Israel in the past continues to save Israel.

We remember how Elijah requests that God take away the burden of his life, and how God responds by turning questions back at Elijah. The dialogue that ensues results in a command – 'Go!' (1 Kgs 19.15). As we found with Job, God answers Job's complaints and accusations with indignant questions. The prophet Isaiah also delivers a word from God that forms a string of questions:

> Woe to you who strive with your Maker,
> earthen vessels with the potter!
> Does the clay say to the one who fashions it, 'What are you making?'
> or 'Your work has no handles?'
> Woe to anyone who says to a father, 'What are you begetting?'
> or to a woman, 'With what are you in labour?'
> Thus says the LORD, the Holy One of Israel, and its Maker:
> Will you question me about my children,
> or command me concerning the work of my hands? (Isa. 45.9–11)

Our Questions, God's Questions

My mother used to say that I shouldn't answer a question with a question. It never occurred to me at the time to ask a further question: if Jesus did it, why shouldn't I? I am not sure that would have earned me any points in my childish attempts to avoid my mother's own questions.

As we have seen, our complaints and questions to God often tell us more about ourselves than they do about God. We find this to be true again in the story of Jesus Stilling the Storm (Mk 4.35–41). Often, we take this story to be about the way we refer to it: Jesus stills a storm. We sympathize with the disciples: how dare Jesus sleep during such a crisis? Can a human really make a wind storm cease? To be sure, this story is about these things, but it is more. It is also a series of questions.

The first important detail in the story is the setting: the sea of Galilee. Throughout the Bible, seas represent danger, chaos, death. We saw how at creation God tames the waters by making the dry land: 'And God said, "Let the waters under the sky be gathered together into one place, and let the dry land appear"' (Gen. 1.9). The land then becomes the space that God provides as a safe dwelling for the land creatures protected from the raging waters. This is an act of God's merciful providence.

In our story in Mark 4, we read that a storm threatens to sink the disciples' little boat. They are nearly overcome with fear. Jesus is with them, but he is sleeping on a cushion. They seem indignant that he is sleeping in spite of their panic. They wake Jesus. He then calms the storm. But rather than being governed by the plot line as sketched out here, this little narrative is structured on a short interchange of questions between the disciples and Jesus.

The first question is from the disciples to Jesus. It is not about the storm, or the condition of the boat, or whether the storm had been expected. In their terror, they ask: 'Lord, do you not care that we are perishing?' (v. 38). It is a question about Jesus' providence and mercy. It is a question not so much about Jesus' expected actions, but about his identity and his relation to them: 'Who are you that you don't seem to care about us?' 'Were we mistaken to think you cared?'

Jesus answers their question with three actions. He wakes up, he rebukes the wind and he calms the sea: 'Peace! Be still!' Then he turns a question at them: 'Why are you afraid? Have you still no faith?' This is not a matter of simple curiosity. Jesus wants to know who the disciples are in relation to him. 'Who are you that you fear when I am with you?'

The disciples' response to Jesus is then a question to each other about him. It is explicitly about his identity and his relation to the rest of the world. 'Who then is this, that even the wind and the sea obey him?' (v. 41). Their response tells us that they are beginning to 'get it', but only slowly. They are beginning to understand that Jesus is the God of creation, the one who made the dry land as a refuge for us and all the creatures in the midst of the waters of death.

Jesus is the same One who calms the floods and sets Noah's little ark safely on the dry land. He is the same One who leads Israel through the Red Sea waters to safety. He is the same One from whose side at the crucifixion flow the waters of life that rescue us from the waters of death. There is a 'fit' between Jesus' identity and his action. And there is a similar 'fit' between Jesus' own identity and action and that of the God of Israel.

It is sometimes true with us as well that our questions about God's relationship to us in our suffering often get turned back on us. We ask about Jesus' identity *vis-à-vis* us: 'Do you not care that we are perishing?' We don't really care who he is in himself. We only want to know how he is going to be good for us. This is entirely appropriate, because that is who Jesus is: for us – *pro nobis*. Nevertheless, we get by way of response to our questions a question about our own identity in relation to him.

Maybe in our own complaints to God we, like the disciples, have the direction reversed. Instead of asking who God is for us, we might do well to ask who we are in relation to God. Sometimes we learn that our identity is in our will to love God in spite of what God sets before us, as was the case with Job. If we are looking to explain why bad things happen to good people, and how justice reigns in the cosmos, we will not find the Bible to be a satisfying compendium of information. We find answers only as we learn what it means to live before and with this God as we suffer.

'Do you care that we are perishing?' That is often our own question we ask the Lord in times of trial. And it is a perfectly appropriate question. If the disciples asked it in a panic, should we not ask it from within our own leaky boats? It is not the fact of our question that is a problem. The problem comes when we turn our question 'Do you not care?' to a resolved declaration: 'God is not there at all.' Petulant statements about God's nature can consume us and choke our cries to the God who listens even as alien presence. When we cease to address God, we cut ourselves off from God's response, and along with it from God's transforming presence. At his last earthly moment, as Jesus ascends to the Father, he answers the disciples with a final statement about his own identity. It is indeed about him being for them and *pro nobis*, for us. It is an answer that rings through all time, down even to us: 'I am with you always ...' (Mt. 28.20). And so the bush that has God in it, though it may burn, will not be consumed. And though our ship be tossed, it will not sink.

Questions for further reflection

- Has God ever addressed you in silence? If so, what was your experience of this, and how did you respond?

- 'Though the fig tree does not blossom, and no fruit is on the vines; though the produce of the olive fails and the fields yield no food; though the flock is cut off from the fold and there is no herd in the stalls, yet I will rejoice in the LORD; I will exult in the God of my salvation' (Hab. 3.17–18). Is this attitude toward God's providence possible for us to embrace today? Why or why not? What does this say about our identity before God?

- When you enter times of loss and you cry out questions to God, what questions will God ask you? What do you hope will be your responses to God's questions?

6

Second Watch: God's Presence When All is Dark

LORD, do not rebuke me in your anger;
do not punish me in your wrath.
Have pity on me, LORD, for I am weak;
heal me, LORD, for my bones are racked.
My spirit shakes with terror;
how long, O LORD, how long?
Turn, O LORD, and deliver me;
save me for your mercy's sake.
For in death no one remembers you;
and who will give you thanks in the grave?
I grow weary because of my groaning;
every night I drench my bed
and flood my couch with tears.
My eyes are wasted with grief

and worn away because of all my enemies.
Depart from me, all evildoers,
for the LORD has heard the sound of my weeping.
The LORD has heard my supplication;
the LORD accepts my prayer.
All my enemies shall be confounded and quake with fear;
they shall turn back and suddenly be put to shame.

PSALM 6

God's Presence and the Nature of Faith

I have noticed that the secular world seems to take it as a given that people of faith have no questions. We have seen that this is not the case. The nature and experience of Christian confession is not immune to the experience of doubt. Our faith is not a simple matter of cognitive assent to certain propositions of Christian teaching (or what we call 'doctrine'). Liturgical traditions include the recitation of historic creeds as part of worship, and creeds certainly do contain 'propositions' or truth claims. But even there, the larger context is worship, not debate. Christian faith does not boil down to a set of statements about God's possible existence.

At the centre of our faith is, as we have seen, a relationship of trust and faithfulness before the presence of the Triune God in Jesus of Nazareth. The Christian Gospel has to do with the practice of living faithfully at the foot of the Cross even in a world filled with pain, vulnerability, suffering and darkness. Who would not stand quaking in one's boots from time to time before the Holy One of Israel? Who does not at some point dwell in the Valley of the Shadow?

But we are told that God is with us even there. That even there God is with us and will lead us by the hand. That God is present with us even in that valley. That God scatters evil: 'For you are not a God who takes pleasure in wickedness, and evil cannot dwell with you' (Ps. 5.4). However, we do not always experience God's presence this way.

It seems as though the secular world caricatures our faith as though it were some sort of talisman to ward off evil, that if found deficient, should be cast aside. But maybe that is what we have made of it. Maybe our God is too small, and we are too large. But if we were large and our God were small, how would He meet us even in suffering? And yet that is exactly what happens on Good Friday.

Almighty God, whose most dear Son went not up to joy but first he suffered pain, and entered not into glory before he was crucified: Mercifully grant that we, walking in the way of the cross, may find it none other than the way of life and peace; through Jesus Christ your Son our Lord. Amen. (Collect for Friday, BCP, p. 99)

Years ago, a non-Christian friend of mine who had many health complications shared with me her fear of death. She told me that she wished she had my faith as a comfort. I reassured her that my faith was neither a problem-solving device nor a self-help programme, nor did it remove my own suffering. I told her that it did give me the strength and indeed the responsibility to face my own pain in faithfulness even through and beyond whatever personal agony I may encounter. I told her that my faith does give me hope to face the hour of my own death without fear, because I trust that God will be present even there.

> I will lead the blind by a road they do not know, by paths they have not known I will guide them. I will turn the darkness before them into light, the rough places into level ground. These are the things I will do, and I will not forsake them. (Isa. 42.16)

But as I realized later, if my friend had really and truly wanted to have my faith, she might have accepted my invitation to seek God in Scripture, prayer and worship. Like a modern-day Nicodemus or Joseph of Arimathea, she could not approach the Lord other than in a very oblique way. In actual fact, she was keeping Jesus at a distance. She did not really want his presence at all. She did not really want my faith. We all have that choice to make.

Even Israel has experienced this deep despair throughout its history. God's presence had been promised and even sometimes perceived and celebrated. But sometimes God seemed to give no apparent response to their cry. Even the prophets, whose task is to mediate God's address to the people, sometimes have nothing to say: 'They shall all cover their lips, for there is no answer from God' (Mic. 3.7). The sins of the people sometimes distort faithfulness to God, and God gives no response at all. Sheer silence. But God's silence is due to humanity's infidelity. God's usual conversation with His people is silenced when His people stray.

'Consider My Servant, Job'

We met Job in the previous chapter, and here we will learn more of him and his response to God. Job has become an icon of suffering even for a secular culture that knows relatively little about the Bible. He is a fascinating character: even though he suffers, yet he lives. Even though God allows Satan to try to crush him, Job puts up with, indeed clings to, that very God. Job encounters the alien presence of God as a familiar absence. Job is deafened by the silence of God. But if all we find in the figure of Job is an exemplar of human suffering, as do so many both outside and inside the Church, we undercut the narrative force of the whole book.

Many read the book of Job looking for answers to the 'problem' of suffering. However, the real 'problem' is that there is no such thing as abstract suffering. Pain is always personal. While suffering is a universal human problem, it is a personal concrete experience. This is why ultimately no one can build an argument to explain why the good suffer.

There is no theory of suffering in the book of Job. The pain experienced there is Job's own pain in the context of his own life and his own loss. The theme of the book is not suffering in general, but Job's own personal response in the midst of his own devastating loss. But the book of Job is about more than just Job's own suffering. Ultimately, it is about the identity of Jesus.

If we were making a film about the identity of Jesus, we would have to shoot at least three scenes. One would be the Bethlehem crèche scene where God is born in human flesh, Mother Mary laying the baby gently in the trough of straw where the cattle had just finished their supper. The second scene would be Golgotha's darkness at noon, with Jesus' screams as he cried out to God in agony and abandonment. These two moments of Jesus' life, the beginning and the end of his own earthly life, define his identity such that Jesus will be recognizable at the goal of the whole story. The third and crowning scene is his triumph:

the resurrection. This scene caps the other two, holding them together and everything in between. Jesus' identity becomes crisp and clear at the resurrection. But the resurrection is itself unimaginable. None of the canonical gospels depict the actual moment. The scene would be impossible to film. Like the evangelists, we would have to focus instead on Jesus' post-resurrection appearances: the Road to Emmaus, breakfast on the beach, Bible study, examining wounds, etc.

But what of Job? What is his identity in relation to God? First and foremost we must recognize the fact that the author at the very beginning of the book implies that Job is a Gentile, a non-Jew. He apparently does not belong to the covenant people. Gentiles are 'aliens from the commonwealth of Israel, and strangers to the covenants of promise, having no hope and without God in the world' (Eph. 2.12). Job seems to be one of these aliens.

Even more surprisingly, despite all that he suffers at the hand of God and even in his fully justified lament and groaning, Job remains bound to the God of Israel. If we neglect this detail, we miss the thrust of the book. The fact of Job's religious status as non-elect shapes the story of God's encounter with Job, and the nature of Job's response.

Even though Job's plight is beyond endurable, he himself remains righteous. 'In spite of being right I am counted a liar; my wound is incurable, though I am without transgression' (34.6). Job the Gentile remains steadfastly faithful to the covenant in which he is not even a welcome guest. Despite this, God calls him 'my servant'. God knows that Job is steadfast. How? Why? We are not told.

Like Elijah, Job suffers. Like Elijah, Job complains to God. But these are very different characters. They each occupy different and distinctive places in the narrative of the people of Israel. Indeed, Elijah was a prophet of Israel in the midst of national apostasy. But, as we have noticed, Job is not identified as an Israelite at all.

The book itself opens with the simple statement that Job is a man 'in the land of Uz'. This is the first hint that we are not dealing with historical narrative. We are missing the usual introductory formula ('There once was a man ...'). Instead, we find something more like 'A man there was ...'[15] This means that there is no clear-cut beginning to the story. It does not follow an earlier story about this man from Uz. Unlike Jesus, Job might as well be a mythical character.

We do not even learn Job's name before the narrator tells us where he lives. More importantly, we are not told where he is from. The text simply says 'there once was a man *in* the land of Uz ...' Job is *in* the land of Uz, but he is not described as being *from* the land of Uz. Job has not come *out from* Uz to where he is now, wherever that may be. Job is introduced to us without mention of origin, fatherland, lineage. For Hebrew narrative, this is indeed odd. But this is not Hebrew narrative.

As we have said, it is more like myth. Job is a Melchizedek-like figure.[16] Usually in Scripture, character descriptions are rich with detail. But Job just *is*, he is in the land of Uz. And as we have seen, names are very important in Scripture. Yet we learn Job's name only after the narrator mentions the odd land where he lives.

Uz itself is not mentioned with frequency in the Bible. Where it does appear, we find it in the company of 'mixed peoples', that is, Jews and Gentiles (cf. Jer. 25.20). Whether Uz indicates Edom or Arabia or some other location we simply do not know. One thing the narrator does tell us is that Uz is 'in the east' (1.3), and that is more significant than anything. The East indicates a land beyond Israel. Job is in a land outside of the boundaries of the covenant people. He is not introduced to us in any way that we might recognize him to be among the twelve tribes of Israel. Job's outsider status is key to grasping the true horror of the book: he suffers under, yet is faithful to, the God of a people among whom he is an alien. The fact that Job is not of the covenant people makes his endurance and fidelity to the God of Israel all the more astounding, even revolting.

The names of God that we find in the book of Job cast even more light on this element. As a literary work, Job is composed of two main genres: narrative and poetic. In the narrative material we find stories about Job and his family, about God and Satan. These are found in the 'bookend' chapters 1–2 and 32–42.

In the poetic material (3–31) in the middle of the book, we find the speeches of Job's friends and Job's responses.

As we know, YHWH is the proper Name of God revealed to Moses on Horeb in Exodus 3.15. In English we represent this name by the word LORD. But in the book of Job, this name appears with only a few exceptions in the narrative frame at the beginning and the end. In the poetic material between these narrative bookends, the Tetragrammaton disappears. The names for God used there are among the generic names for God we find throughout the Bible, such as *Elohim* (God), *El Shaddai* (the Almighty), and so on. It is YHWH, the proper name of the covenant God, that at the beginning of the book identifies the God who gives Job over to Satan in a wager. And it is YHWH who at the end of the book answers Job out of the whirlwind. Job contends with YHWH, the LORD God of Israel. That is clear. But why Job puts up with YHWH is another question entirely.

> If I go forward, he is not there;
> or backward, I cannot perceive him;
> on the left he hides, and I cannot behold him;
> I turn to the right, but I cannot see him.
> But he knows the way that I take;
> when he has tested me, I shall come out like gold.
> My foot has held fast to his steps;
> I have kept his way and have not turned aside.

I have not departed from the commandment of his lips;

I have treasured in my bosom the words of his mouth. (Job
23.8–12)

We must let the LORD answer our earlier question 'Who is Job?'
In his conversation with Satan, the LORD identifies this man
from the East twice as 'my servant Job' (1.8; 2.3). This designation
is repeated at the end of the story (42.7-8). The identification of
Job as the LORD's servant bookends the poetic material.

Not only is Job the LORD's servant, but the LORD hands Job
over to Satan to prove that 'there is none like (Job)' in integrity
and faithfulness. In the face of Satan, the LORD God of Israel
offers up His own servant Job, the man in the East, as a paragon
of strength, virtue and covenant faithfulness.

But how does the LORD know that Job is his servant? We are
not given any evidence for Job's righteousness or servanthood
other than the LORD's simple statement declaring him so. There
is no narrated interaction between the two which would give
us a hint of a relationship before the LORD declares this. The
only detail we have is that the LORD seems to entrust His own
righteousness before Satan to the character and person of this
man Job. Maybe it is simply this that makes the LORD confident
that Job is His servant.

Satan has taunted the LORD in this discernment of Job's
character. Satan suggests that the reason Job is the LORD's servant

is simply that Job has received blessing from the LORD's hand. 'You have blessed the work of his hands, and his possessions have increased in the land. But stretch out your hand now, and touch all that he has, and he will curse you' (1.9–11).[17]

The LORD responds: 'Very well, all he has is in your power; only do not stretch out your hand against him' (1.12; cf. 2.6). The LORD has vouched for Job's faithful service, putting His own reputation into the hands of a mortal who, in human weakness, may well prove to be no righteous man at all. Satan, the Accuser, would have 'won' the wager, proving the LORD a fool.

We might ask a prior question: what was Satan doing in the 'presence of the LORD' in the first place (1.12b; cf. 2.7)? Satan simply appears there as if out of nowhere, in the heavenly council no less (1.6). Satan does not belong there. The LORD does not ask Satan why he has come, but He does ask what Satan has been doing with his time. Satan answers that he has been 'going to and fro on the earth and walking up and down on it' (1.7). He has just been poking around, scoping out the joint.

The LORD points to Job for Satan's consideration even before Satan asks any questions. Why does He draw Satan's attention to Job? It is as though He is proud of His servant. The quality of the servant makes a statement about the master. The LORD knows this: Job's righteousness is a reflection on the LORD's righteousness. But this itself puts the LORD in a vulnerable position *vis-à-vis* His Adversary. He has put His own sovereignty in the hands of this man, Job, who is not even of the LORD's covenant people. It is a two-way relationship: Job has made himself vulnerable in trusting this foreign God.

Satan plays a major role in the beginning of the book, but seems to recede into the wings beginning with the poetic mid-section of the book. It strikes us that during Job's laments, he does not complain to Satan. He does not curse Satan. He does not even address Satan. And Satan does not return in the closing narrative section of the book. Even though it is Satan who has afflicted Job, it is the LORD who is Job's adversary at this point (30.21). It is only the LORD who allowed this suffering. It is only before the LORD that Job pours lament. It is only to the LORD that Job clings.

Even so, Job does not recognize the LORD in his suffering. The LORD becomes alien to Job, even as Job himself is an alien, this servant of the LORD from the East:

> I cry to you and you do not answer me; I stand, and you merely look at me. You have turned cruel to me; with the might of your hand you persecute me. (30.20–21)

Job does not doubt that God blesses, for he know it is God's role to bless. Yet Job does not curse God. He only curses his own life. 'I loathe my life; I will give free utterance to my complaint; I will speak in the bitterness of my soul' (10.1). And yet this does not keep Job from petitioning God to be true to Himself. The LORD is the one who creates in blessing, and Job reminds Him: 'Does it seem good to you to oppress, to despise the work of your hands and favour the schemes of the wicked?' (10.3). How then can this be the LORD? For this very reason Job cannot see his God. He cannot discern Him.

> He has kindled his wrath against me, and counts me as his adversary. His troops come on together; they have thrown up siegeworks against me, and encamp around my tent. He has put my family far from me, and my acquaintances are wholly estranged from me. (19.11–13; cf. Ps. 88.19)

God's wrath and curse have truly replaced His kindness and blessing. It does not merely seem this way. It is this way. God is not confronting Job in the guise of curse and wrath, as though this were a staged play. God truly has allowed Job to be cast into darkness and terror. God has allowed this. And yet it is even in that darkness and terror that Job cries out to this alien God. Here we find a foretaste of Jesus' cry of dereliction: God has indeed abandoned him.

This fact nearly drives Job mad: God is with Job, but is unrecognizable, an alien, as if not present at all. Yet Job never doubts that it is before this very God that he stands: 'Why do you hide your face, and count me as your enemy? Will you frighten a windblown leaf and pursue dry chaff?' (13.24–25). Even so, Job trusts God and accepts Him in this completely incomprehensible form: 'Though He slay me, yet will I trust in Him: but I will maintain mine own ways before Him' (13.15, KJV). Job does not curse, but neither does Job let go in his struggle.

Like Jacob wrestling with the divine figure at the Jabbok, Job wrestles with God and will not let go. It is especially after Satan has him in his grasp that Job shows his true colours. It is then that he proves the LORD right, that he is indeed the servant of the LORD, that he is in fact 'blameless and upright, honouring God and turning away from evil' (1.8). After Job loses his children, his servants and his herds, any reader unfamiliar with the biblical canon would expect Job to give up. He has become mad, this man from the East. He mourns as would a faithful Israelite, and he even worships the God who allowed this suffering.

> Then Job arose, tore his robe, shaved his head, and fell on the ground and worshipped ... Naked I came from my mother's womb, and naked shall I return there; the LORD gave, and the LORD has taken away; blessed be the name of the LORD. (1.20–21)

This question Job responds to is also ours, and we in our day must choose our own response. The question is not will we suffer loss?

Of course we will suffer loss and pain. The question rather is this: how will we respond? The blessings of God are freely showered upon us. If they weren't free, they would not be blessings. They would be expectations. They would be wages earned. Asking God to justify Himself when these blessings dry up reveals our fundamental assumptions. For some strange reason, we think God owes us something.

And our questions about suffering are not finally about God, but about us. This is the case with Job. His questions to God become questions back at Job: 'Where were you when ...?' We ourselves have a choice in how we respond to suffering. We can choose light and life, or darkness and death. Which will it be: grace, or doom?

In the poetic sections that form the core of the book of Job, we find that Wisdom is known to God alone. Speculation about it will yield no truth. Indeed, there is no point even in asking about Wisdom, apart from directly addressing the One who is Wisdom. The fact that humans and all other creatures know nothing of Wisdom is painful enough to face. The fact that hell and death have heard of it seems ironic at best, and the height of cruelty at worst. Only God understands the way to it.

But where shall wisdom be found? And where is the place of understanding? Mortals do not know the way to it, and it is not found in the land of the living ... It is hidden from the eyes of all living, and concealed from the birds of the air. Abaddon and

Death say, 'We have heard a rumour of it with our ears.' God understands the way to it ... And he said to humankind, 'Truly, the fear of the LORD that is wisdom; and to depart from evil is understanding.' (Job 28.12–13, 21–23, 28)

Job's friends have an air of superiority in their speeches to him. And they *are* superior to him, insofar as they are outside and beyond the muck and the agony and the crushing pain that Job faces. When they are dismayed by Job's complaints, they utter judgements about the suffering of those who deserve it. But they themselves are totally unaffected by Job's own suffering. They don't see themselves this way; they seem to think that they are in solidarity with Job. But they operate under the implicit assumption that the pious will someday reap their reward from the Almighty. This is not the God of Job's struggle. The LORD God of Israel is free and unfettered in His relationship to creation. This God is not bound by the logic of *do ut des*: I give to you so that you will give to me.

The clichés and passé formulae that Job's friends dish out to him in his agony betray their assumptions that the world follows a universal moral order. But in Job's afflictions as well as in his responses, his friends are confronted with the fact that such order is not the way of the Almighty, the LORD God. So they are shocked, even offended, by Job's responses when Job is doggedly faithful and when he is alarmingly sacrilegious as well.

The God of Job's friends is the God of the Deists. This is the God who creates and then stands back at a remove. This is the God of those who feel His ways need defending, who construct theories of why God allows good people to suffer. This is the God whose ways ultimately cannot be defended, who must be attacked and denied, indeed blotted out. We hear this even from very pious people: 'Of course, *my* God would never do such a thing.' The question to this statement is: 'Where you do find such a god?' The answer is: inside themselves. Job's friends are these pious people. The God of Job's friends could never act freely. Their God could only act within the bounds of their own assumptions about what counts for what their God should or should not do, could or could not do. Their God could never do anything *gratis*, freely and graciously. Their God is very small.

But the God of Job's friends is not the God with whom Job struggles. Their God is not the LORD God of Israel. Their God is neither the Lord of the Nativity, nor of the Cross, nor of the Empty Tomb.

Job as Witness to Christ

As with other figures from the Old Testament, Job has the vocation of witnessing to Christ. In Job's freedom before God, he travels through the hell of searing pain and yet remains in agonizing struggle with this absent God, an absence from which Job refuses to flee. Just as Christ will do, Job remains faithful to the end. And just as Jesus' own suffering is a necessary element of his identity, so is Job's suffering of his identity. We recognize Job's God when we hear Jesus say:

> Oh, how foolish you are, and how slow of heart to believe all that the prophets have declared! Was it not necessary that the Messiah should suffer these things and then enter into his glory? (Lk. 24.25–26)

On his own eighth day, as a type of Christ, at the end of the book Job participates by foretaste in the resurrection. He receives the blessing of his stolen joy returned to him, in overabundance: 'The LORD blessed the latter days of Job more than his beginning' (42.12ff.; cf. 1.2ff.). His daughters are the most beautiful in the land. In the days when daughters were an economic liability, Job's daughters are remarkable. Like the daughters of Zelophehad (Num. 27.7) Job's daughters also are given their own inheritance (Job 42.15). This is unheard of elsewhere in the Bible.

And yet this restoration is not complete restoration at all. Job's first wife and children are not brought back to life or raised from the dead. His family is not reconstituted. While Job is indeed a blessed man at the end of the story, he is not the same man. It is not as if God picks him up, dusts him off and says 'There, there; all better now.' Job's controversy with God has not vanished as though a bad dream.

In this also, Job is a type of Jesus Christ.[18] Jesus' abandonment on the cross is not an illusion. It is real. His resurrection is not a resuscitation, a return to his former life in his earthly flesh. In his resurrected body Jesus is recognizable as the one with whom the disciples ate, learned and travelled, but it is a recognition that is hard won. Only after the message of the angels at the empty tomb, Jesus' breaking of the bread and the opening of the Scriptures, after Thomas' examining of the wounds, only then do the disciples realize it is their old friend Jesus, their 'Lord and God' (Jn. 20.28). Jesus is the same one, and yet not the same one at all. The torture of the crucifixion and the cry of dereliction remain. They are not erased.

In this manner, Job retains the wounds of his own suffering and the blessings of his own steadfastness. Job not only witnesses to Jesus Christ, but he also is a figure pointing to the vocation of Christians yet to come. We too may be put to such a trial, to remain face to face before the God who seems absent even as alien presence. And what will our response be?

Job's unexpected (and seemingly unwarranted) faithfulness to the God of Israel stuns us. This God has allowed Satan to grind Job's face into the dirt. Why does Job not give up on this terrible God? He would be justified to heed his wife: 'Curse God and die' (Job 2.9). This is just one of the ways Job functions as a witness to Christ: he remains faithful even in great suffering and loss. But, unlike Jesus, Job does not go to his own death. Unlike Jesus, Job is spared that. The LORD refuses to allow Satan that much: 'Very well, all that he has is in your power; only do not stretch out your hand against him' (Job 1.12).

As type, Job both points to Christ and participates in Christ, even to his cry of dereliction: 'Why have you abandoned me?' (Ps. 22.1). Jesus' cry of dereliction is even more horrific for us to hear than Job's response to the news of the loss of his entire family. But Job's response is among one of the harshest verses in the Bible.

> Then Job arose, tore his robe, shaved his head, and fell on the ground and worshipped. He said, 'Naked I came from my mother's womb, and naked shall I return there; the LORD gave, and the LORD has taken away; blessed be the name of the LORD.' In all this Job did not sin or charge God with wrong-doing. (1.20–22)

Throughout his trials, Job never curses God. Instead, Job curses the day he was born. Job knows that the LORD God of Israel is free, and that this freedom embraces both giving and taking away. This freedom will become even more startling in God's self-emptying in the Incarnation and bleeding on the Cross.

'My God, My God, Why Have You Abandoned Me?'

In his experience of righteous suffering, Job is a type of Christ. And yet, while Job's own life is spared, Jesus does indeed truly die. Jesus is indeed actually forsaken. It doesn't just seem that way. It is that way. On the cross, God self-empties in abandoning Jesus, and abandons His own identity as the One who has been present. Jesus' cry of dereliction is not simply the voice of a devout Jew reciting Psalms. He is in actual fact forsaken by God in a way that Job was not. God's presence has turned into God's absence. So there is a likeness yet unlikeness between Job and Jesus.

Surprisingly enough, we find a fit also between God's act of creating and Jesus' cry of dereliction. This means that Creation itself is a type of Redemption.[19] God's calling the world into being is a type of Jesus' crying out in abandonment. Redemption does not cancel creation – it perfects it. The first does not undo the second. In both, love and self-emptying are joined. The One who called the world into being now empties himself in a 'creative act of self-constriction'.[20] The modern Jewish mystic, French intellectual and near-convert to Catholicism Simone Weil puts it this way:

> Creation is abdication ... the apparent absence of God in this world is the actual reality of God ... Not only the Passion but the Creation itself is a renunciation and sacrifice on the

part of God ... If God did not abandon [created things], they would not exist. His presence would annul their existence as a flame kills a butterfly.[21]

The God of creation; the God of Abraham, Isaac and Jacob; the LORD of Moses; the God of Job; Jesus Christ himself: these are all one and the same God. Creation and the cry of dereliction are not magnets turned back-to-back opposing or repelling one another. Creation as presence and dereliction as absence each draw the other into its field of power. Each fits the other. Darkness is not in itself evil. God divides the day from the night, and the darkness does not struggle against God. According to the creation account, God does not call darkness into being, but has complete control over it. He simply separates the light out from it ('And God separated the Light from the Darkness', Gen. 1.4).

And God is present even in the darkness. The relationship between darkness and light is not a battle in progress, whose results we await. God has already won.

Where can I go then from your Spirit?
Where can I flee from your presence?
If I climb up to heaven, you are there;
if I make the grave my bed, you are there also.
If I take the wings of the morning
and dwell in the uttermost parts of the sea,

Even there your hand will lead me

And your right hand hold me fast.

If I say, 'Surely the darkness will cover me,

And the light around me turn to night.'

Darkness is not dark to you;

The night is as bright as the day;

Darkness and light to you are both alike. (Ps. 139.6–9)

Even the darkness is subject to God's light. There is no balance here yet to be tipped. This confession is expressed in the Morning Prayer Collect for Renewal of Life:

O God, the King eternal, who divides the day from the night and turns the shadow of death into the morning: Drive far from us all wrong desires, incline our hearts to keep your law, and guide our feet into the way of peace; that, having done your will with cheerfulness while it was day, we may, when night comes, rejoice to give you thanks; through Jesus Christ our Lord. Amen. (BCP p. 99)

Darkness is not the opposite of light. It is simply the lack of light. So also evil is not the opposite of good. Rather, evil is the absence of good. God's blessing is presence. Evil is void, emptiness.

We prepare ourselves during Lent for the Light of Easter, a light so strong it may blind our eyes rather than simply illuminate our path. Here is the rub: the Christian faith is not a project to be constructed. It is a life to be lived. It is not a concept. It is a relationship. Our objections to innocent suffering are and should be many. These objections are fully acceptable and expected in the sight of God. But, as we look on human suffering, Christians behold the wounds of the crucified Christ. And the Christian cannot behold Christ and his wounds apart from hearing the promise of the risen Christ at his Ascension: 'I am with you always.'

Questions for further reflection

- 'Though he slay me, yet will I trust in Him' (Job 13.15, KJV). Discuss.
- How would you answer the question 'Do you ever have doubts about the Christian faith?'
- What would you offer a friend who says she wishes she had your faith?

7

Third Watch: Dawn

Then one of the elders addressed me, saying, 'Who are these, robed in white, and where have they come from?' I said to him, 'Sir, you are the one that knows.' Then he said to me, 'These are they who have come out of the great ordeal; they have washed their robes and made them white in the blood of the Lamb. For this reason they are before the throne of God, and worship him day and night within his temple, and the one who is seated on the throne will shelter them. They will hunger no more, and thirst no more; the sun will not strike them, nor any scorching heat; for the Lamb at the centre of the throne will be their shepherd, and he will guide them to springs of the water of life, and God will wipe away every tear from their eyes.'

REV. 7.13–17

Why would we consider martyrs as a sign of God's presence, indeed as the Dawning of a new day? Should they not be better considered as creatures of the Night, experiencing in God's abandonment and absence their Dark Night of the Soul? And if we consider them at the Dawn of the day, are we thereby suggesting that martyrdom is a good unto itself? After all, aren't martyrs really just fanatics? Are we promoting suffering? Are we holding martyrs up as heroes at a level we could never reach, whose vocation is fundamentally different from our own?

Indeed, it seems impossible for those among us who live comfortable lives even to begin to imagine martyrdom. It can seem completely foreign to hear of what Christians elsewhere in the world endure simply in order to confess Christ and walk in his love. And yet reports of such suffering seem to increase with each passing week. But are we not all called to suffering for the name of Christ?

'He Must Increase; I Must Decrease' (Jn 3.30)

The third-century biblical interpreter Origen wrote in the prologue to his *Contra Celsum* about the relationship between Jesus' silence at his trial and our own vocation as his followers. Because Jesus was silent before his accusers during his passion,

Origen says, the responsibility is now on us to be a voice for him. We must not remain silent. But how are we to speak for Christ, to give voice to his own self-offering? Is this what Colossians 1.24 means: supplementing what is left over in Christ's sufferings? Are we to conform our lives to Jesus' own? This sounds horrifying. Jesus' identity is cross-shaped. Is ours meant to be also?

Scripture tells us that our life, when shaped by Jesus' cross, is not affliction without consolation. Affliction bound to the cruciform life is not to be endured as though we were solitary individuals in isolation one from the other. We are one body in Christ. This unity in Christ establishes our unity with each other. This means that as we pass through affliction we participate in Christ, and this is for the wellbeing of all:

> For just as the sufferings of Christ are abundant for us, so also our consolation is abundant through Christ. If we are being afflicted, it is for your consolation and salvation; if we are being consoled, it is for your consolation, which you experience when you patiently endure the same sufferings that we are also suffering. (2 Cor. 1.5–6)

We share this comfort as we participate in the life and death of Christ. When grounded in his, our affliction brings a resurrection of joy that protects us from the powers of death. Even though we may suffer, we are not crushed. Even in our confusion over what seems to be God's absence, we are not driven to complete despair. And by carrying in our bodies the death of Jesus we make visible his life. Each of us is to make evident the power that belongs to God and not to us (2 Cor. 4.7–12). We have the comfort and encouragement of each other in our persecutions (1 Thess. 3.2–3).

Having given testimony with our words and our lives, however, we are not to be hailed as heroes. We have simply done what is required of us as Christians: 'we have done only what we ought to have done!' (Lk. 17.10). For many in the early church, and in some places today, confession and mission require a testimony that may require passing on to others the Gospel by handing over one's very life.

And this is not merely a thing of the past; it is still the case in some areas of the world where the Church is in fact growing despite such affliction. While we Christians in the West may think that Christian martyrdom is no longer a reality, others elsewhere still bear witness through the spilling of their blood. We who have freedom of religion in our laws do not share the sense of urgency of Christian witness they do.

We find the earliest record of Christian martyrdom in Acts 7, where Stephen was stoned for his confession of Jesus. Stephen's sermon proves a terrible offence to the Council and High Priest. It results in their charging him with blasphemy as he describes his vision: '"Look," he said, "I see the heavens opened and the

Son of Man standing at the right hand of God!"' (Acts 7.55–56). Being at the right hand of God is the position of power and authority. We draw from this our expression 'my right-hand man'. Stephen has said the unsayable: a man, namely this Jesus, stands at the right hand of God. The book of Acts tells the story of how the Church went on to spread throughout all the known world of that day.

The Blood of the Martyrs, the Seed of the Church

The third-century North African Church Father Tertullian said that the blood of the martyrs is the seed of the Church. Absorbing hatred in the Name of Jesus by giving over one's own life, the Christian martyr furthers the reconciling work of the Lord. These deeds of self-giving extend the proclamation of the Gospel. Where one might have thought that murder would stifle the voice crying for peace, in actual fact it only amplifies it. This is the logic of the cross, and the paradox of the way those who bear the cross witness to the power of the resurrection. As the Revd Dr Martin Luther King, Jr, once said, 'Darkness cannot drive out darkness; only light can do that. Hate cannot drive out hate; only love can do that.'

The blood of the martyrs remains the seed of the Church. Wherever Christians struggle in this self-giving way for the peace of God, there the Church flourishes. No wonder then that the Church in the West seems weak and nasal-voiced. We know that violence in our fallen world begets further violence. But we seem to have forgotten that violence absorbed into the Name of Christ begets peace and reconciliation. This is in fact the significance of the cross and empty tomb. It may seem counter-intuitive, but the Church's work of reconciliation in the Name is only strengthened as we point, like Paul, to the weakness of the Cross. This weakness is indeed the power of God. Christian martyrs are at the Dawn of the new day because they are the vanguard of the Church. Christian martyrs are therefore at the turn of the ages: 'But in your hearts sanctify Christ as Lord. Always be ready to make your defence to anyone who demands from you an accounting for the hope that is in you' (1 Pet. 3.15).

In his reflections on the Feast of St Thomas à Becket on 29 December 2014 at Canterbury Cathedral, Archbishop Justin Welby spoke of this theme of the martyrs' important witness:

Martyrdom is a concept that needs rescuing. It is to bear witness to the light of Christ at the moment of greatest darkness; when the sword falls, the gun fires, the flames rise, flames of darkness visible – the flames of hell that seek the destruction of all testimony to the goodness of God in Christ ... It has nothing to do with killing others, with crusade or violent campaign. The martyr is light itself, who in one brief moment opens the heavens to those who hear the testimony of death, and changes our sense of time ... In martyrdom time is breached: our perspective that perceives only dark at the end of life is suddenly lit by the martyr's lightning so that we see a long road ahead, not for ever stony and hard, but broad, by a stream accompanied by angels of mercy and sustenance.

The concept of martyrdom needs to be reclaimed. The logical next step would be to suggest that the act itself of martyrdom needs to be reclaimed. After all, one can't separate this particular concept from the particular act.

From whom does martyrdom need reclaiming? From those of us who, lulled by the creature comforts of our lives, may have forgotten its power and its call. From those of us who may not know what it could mean to relinquish anything into the wounds of Christ. In his sermon the Archbishop challenges us to ask what our own martyrdom might mean, our own witness to the Light of Christ. He urges us to heed the Spirit's call to take risks in seeking the cruciform life of discipleship.

Christian martyrs greet the dawn, guard the city, await the sunrise. They know the sun will indeed rise. But they are aware that night is not short. They burn with desire for the rays of morning light. Martyrs yearn for dawn even more than do the exhausted watchmen who have sat sentry throughout the hours of darkness. 'My soul waits for the LORD, more than watchmen for the morning, more than watchmen for the morning' (Ps. 130.5).

Christian martyrs trust that even though the night be long, the darkness be deep and vision be clouded, Jesus' resurrection will usher in the New Creation. Christian martyrs teach us a willingness to trust in God. Embracing all evidence to the contrary, they wait and hope.

Most remarkably, Christian martyrs are people of joy and gratitude. They know their hands are empty, and they trust that God will fill them. This is very difficult for those of us who perceive our hands already to be full. It is simply our expectation that comfort should be the norm.

Our Lenten disciplines are meant to strip us bare of all pretence to fullness. It often takes paring away, either by the disciplines we take on or by the everyday suffering that comes our way, for us to learn that we have been empty all along. Why do we find fullness of life only when we are filled with the blood of Christ?

so that the genuineness of your faith – being more precious than gold that, though perishable, is tested by fire – may be

found to result in praise and glory and honour when Jesus
Christ is revealed. (1 Pet. 1.7)

Christian martyrdom is always to be distinguished from
self-murder. It is never to be sought for fame or glory, as
a means of political protest, out of religious zeal or self-
enlightenment. If there is another way to remain steadfast
in Christian witness, one is to choose that other way. While
it is true that Christian martyrs are bigger in their deaths
than in their lives, Christian martyrdom is never to be
romanticized.

How can we, as we live out our Lenten lives, actually embrace
martyrdom? Many of us live in places where spilling our blood
for the sake of the Name will never become a necessity. But there
is a way, I believe, that we can embrace a cruciform life apart
from this more dramatic form of witness. It is, in fact, quite
imaginable.

Red Martyrs and White Martyrs

As early as the fifth century, the Church Father Jerome made the
now-classic distinction between different types of martyrs. 'Red
martyrs' (or 'wet martyrs') are those who lose their lives for the
sake of the Name; 'white martyrs' (or 'dry martyrs') are those

who unite themselves with Christ, embracing the cruciform life in their own everyday realities life. But for the white martyr their context does not bring on the shedding of their own blood.

This distinction is still a helpful way for us to think about our own confession and witness, especially as we each try in our own context to embrace a full witness to the living Christ. Physical death is not the only way of dying to self. It is our decrease alone that brings the increase of love. St Catherine of Siena in the twelfth century said: 'By how much more a person dies to self, by so much more they live to God.'

Even in the twenty-first century, both red and white martyrs are still being made throughout the world. As I write in February of 2015, atrocities against Christians escalate in Iraq, Syria, Pakistan and North Africa. Just this week twenty-one Egyptian Coptic Christians were martyred in Libya. They refused to renounce their confession. Praying to Jesus on their knees, they were hooded and decapitated by the sword. Nigeria and the Sudan have painfully fresh memories of horrific slaughter of huge numbers, many Christians among them. And in China, Palestine and the Crimea, Christians have their freedoms constricted and proscribed.

Here are just a few examples of white martyrs. In twentieth-century Europe, Reformed Christian and white martyr Corrie ten Boom (1892–1983) was imprisoned for sheltering Jews from the Nazis. She wrote of her witness to Christ in her book *The Hiding*

Place. Like ten Boom, Magda and André Trocmé (1901–1996/ 1901–1971), both church leaders among the French Huguenots, were also imprisoned for hiding Jews during the Third Reich. Their tale is told by historian Philip Hallie in *Lest Innocent Blood Be Shed*. In India, one of the most famous twentieth-century white martyrs is the iconic Mother Teresa of Calcutta (1910–1997) who gave her days to work among the poorest of the poor.

But we do not have to travel to another continent or to face a hostile political regime to learn about suffering. We are human, and it is of the human condition to experience pain and loss. Can we set our own sufferings, puny as they may seem when compared to those of even these white martyrs, at the foot of the cross? Can we lay down our own pain as an offering to Christ and to the Church? Can we too 'rejoice in our sufferings, completing what is lacking in Christ's afflictions for the sake of his body, that is, the church' (Col. 1.24)? We may need to pray hard and think creatively here. But we do not need to look far. We probably know at least one person who has lost friends or family or well-being for the sake of his or her faith.

Here is just a single example of how one woman in twentieth-century North America became, in her own way and her own context, a white martyr: she lost her livelihood because of her Christian confession. She worked for a major chemical company bidding on a contract to develop nerve gas components for market to the US army. The only purpose of these chemical components was to be used to make the gas, and the only purpose of the nerve gas was indiscriminate slaughter. Use of the gas could not be confined to any specific target: no air base, no naval port, no weapons plant. The manufacturers and buyers could not rule out the possibility that the deployment of the gas might result in civilian casualties. Faithful to the Lord of Life, this woman refused to participate in the development of the chemical component of this deadly gas, and she was fired.

Such stories abound, but we do not often think of these people as martyrs. If we understand this kind of witness as white martyrdom, we might be able to see ourselves in places where we too could take up our own cross and lay down our own lives. We need to be looking for places where our own confession requires this kind of costly discipleship.

As for recent red martyrs, their stories are splashed across our media. This probably has more to say about our culture's thirst for violence and horror rather than any genuine concern for Christian martyrs *per se*. But we Christians in the West do not seem outraged by the sufferings of these red martyrs any more than does the general public. Why is this? Maybe we think their suffering is a result of the generic violence of radical extremist movements and political despotism rather than linked to their own confession of Jesus Christ.

It is certainly true that Christians are not the only targets of extremists. Many others fall into their sights, regardless of age, sex, ethnicity, nationality or creed. And certainly we Christians are charged to have compassion on *all* people, whether or not they are brothers and sisters in Christ. The parable of the Good Samaritan would have us see at least that.

But the confession that shapes us into the cruciform life would push us yet further. In our worship, after the reading of Scripture, we acclaim aloud 'the Word/Gospel of the Lord'. If we are sincere in this, how could we not attend seriously to the other places in Scripture that tell us we are to care for each other, specifically within the Body of Christ (Gal. 6.2; Mt. 25.31ff.), because of our unity in him (1 Cor. 12.15–16; John 17)?

A prominent Jewish theologian in the United States expressed his shock to find Christians so lukewarm in their response to these recent and very public martyrdoms. He remarked that if Jews were targets of such violence and degradation, the Jewish people around the world would not remain silent. But most Christians are not of any single ethnicity. Our religious unity is based on Christ, and so it is cross-cultural and inter-ethnic. While a specifically Christian response to Christian persecution might look different from a Jewish response to a specifically Jewish persecution, the keen observation of my Jewish colleague has been convicting.

For Christians especially in the West, who live in countries that wield much political power, a response would at least involve public forms of protest. But we would need to do more. Our theological forms of piety have traditionally been prayer and fasting (Acts 13.3; 14.23). In much of Western Protestantism, fasting in particular has dropped out of practice. But both fasting and prayer would expand the witness of these Christian martyrs through our own bodies, as with a ripple effect. It would allow us to share in their suffering and witness as our lives are further conformed to the cross.

Anglican Martyrs in the Twenty-First Century

Anglican martyrs, both red and white, continue to be made in the twenty-first century. We will consider three Anglican communities where martyrdom is not outside the norm to see what these Christians draw from Scripture to find God's presence in the midst of their very grave affliction. In all three cases there were kidnappings, torture and murder. But the differences among the three in their socio-political contexts are important to note. The Melanesian Brotherhood[22] was by grace free from the mass displacement which was deeply woven into the lives of the other communities we will consider: those in Iraq (St George's parish, Baghdad) and in the Sudan (especially from Bishop Gwynne College in Juba).

Martyrs in the Anglican parish of St George's, Baghdad, were made from the simple fact of their Christian confession, but more especially upon conversion from Islam.[23] In a nation where Islam is the only permitted religion, indeed where the practice of or conversion to any other religion is punishable by death, Christian converts risk their very lives.

The Jieng martyrs of the Sudan bear resemblance to those of Baghdad in so far as their Christian confession itself put their lives at risk.[24] However, the socio-political context in the Sudan included civil war. Also unlike St George's urban parish, the Jieng Christians were in rural areas. At one point the setting was flight from war and a refugee camp.

The martyrs of the Melanesian Brotherhood were also subject to violence at the hand of the state.[25] But the Brothers were martyred not simply for confessing the Name (as though such a thing could be simple), but also for consistently living out their vocation of peace-making in the Name. This was a vocation carefully discerned. While some of the Brothers were indeed red martyrs, those who supported them and still live to tell their stories are white martyrs. The work of the white martyrs for reconciliation and peace can teach us as we try to discern what white martyrdom might mean for us in our own socio-political context.

But first, let us look at how each community finds God's presence in Scripture, and how members face their fears and doubts with faith that God is present. Certainly, each of these will be important for us in any kind of Christian witness, whether ours actually reaches the status of white martyrdom or not.

God's Presence in Scripture

Each of these communities draws great strength from corporate worship and from Scripture. One of the passages that held deep significance both for St George's, Baghdad, and also for the Jieng Sudanese Christians, is the story of the fiery furnace in Daniel 3. The three Hebrew youths in this story, Shadrach, Meshach and Abednego, are among the exiles in Babylon. They refuse to bow down to an idol and are summarily bound and thrown into the fiery furnace by King Nebuchadnezzar. The servants of the king then report that the three young men are walking unbound in the flames unharmed, along with a fourth figure.

This image of the youths in the fiery furnace has also been important throughout the history of Christian art and biblical interpretation. This is true particularly among communities persecuted for their confession. In the catacombs of Rome, where persecuted Christians held their prayers in hiding, we find a third-century painting of the scene of the fiery furnace. In the history of biblical interpretation, the fourth figure discerned among the flames along with Shadrach, Meshach and Abednego is often understood to be Christ. God enters the flames of persecution and is present with His suffering people. The celebration of Easter Vigil in the Eastern traditions includes a reading from Daniel 3. Here the story of the three-plus-one individuals in the fiery furnace is taken to be a vision of Christ's descent into hell, whence he draws Adam and Eve from its flames.

There was apparently a mural in the Sudan's Khartoum Museum depicting this scene, a testimony to the faith of the Nubian Christians in ancient times who inhabited the area now occupied by Sudan. Marc Nikkel designed a mural of this story in 1986 for the Chapel at Bishop Gwynne College in the Sudan where he taught. No wonder, then, that this scene comes to the fore in some of the Jieng poems and prayers.

The scene of the three youths accompanied by the fourth figure in the fiery flames is important also to the Christians of St George's, Baghdad. They find God's presence even in the fires of persecution just as Christ was present to Shadrach, Meshach and Abednego. This is true certainly because of the intensity of their own persecution but also because of their specific cultural and geographical context. And St George's Canon Andrew White tells a story of one Christmas morning when, as he recounted the birth of Jesus in Bethlehem, a little boy in the congregation exclaimed that 'Jesus did not first go to Bethlehem! He came here to Iraq – He was in the flames with Shadrach, Meshach and Abednego.'[26]

Other themes from Scripture which feed the souls of the Christians of St George's include those of exile and return. A psalm that they found nurturing was Psalm 137. As Canon White notes, this is generally understood to have been composed during Judah's exile in present-day Iraq. It therefore has a special place in the heart of the people of St George's:

> By the waters of Babylon we sat down and wept,
>
> when we remembered you, O Zion.
>
> As for our harps, we hung them up
>
> on the trees in the midst of that land.
>
> For those who led us away captive asked us for a song,
>
> and our oppressors called for mirth:
>
> 'Sing us one of the songs of Zion.'
>
> How shall we sing the LORD's song
>
> upon an alien soil? (Ps. 137.1–4)

St George's, of course, has many congregants who are originally from Baghdad but who because of their faith feel exiled in their own land. Even by their own waters of Babylon, in their own exile, they sing the LORD's song despite great danger. They consistently seek God's presence even in their exile and seeming abandonment, singing songs of Zion even as aliens on their own soil.

Scripture texts such as those that speak of the unity of the Body, such as 1 Corinthians 12, undergird their ability to endure persecution. The corporate nature of their experience of God's presence was nourishing to their faith and endurance. They were strengthened in each other, knowing that they are not just a conglomerate of individuals. Rather, they are the body of Christ there in Baghdad. God's presence in their suffering is understood corporately: 'If one member suffers, all suffer together ... You are the Body of Christ, and individually members of it' (1 Cor. 12.26–27). In addition, the high priestly prayer in John 17 reminds them that they are one with Jesus just as the Son and the Father are one.

For the Jieng Christians in Sudan among whom Marc Nikkel worked, texts with themes of refuge even in alienation and estrangement also brought solace: 'I hate those who cling to worthless idols, and I put my trust in the LORD' (Ps. 31.6). In the West we are often put off by such texts because they sound harsh and even offensive to our ears. However, when one's own daily reality is harsh, it may be comforting to hear that even such bitterness is within God's embrace.

Some of the most important texts for the Melanesian Brotherhood are from the Sermon on the Mount in Matthew 5–7, and in particular the Beatitudes:

Blessed are the poor in spirit, for theirs is the kingdom of heaven.

Blessed are those who mourn, for they will be comforted.

Blessed are the meek, for they will inherit the earth.

Blessed are those who hunger and thirst for righteousness, for they will be filled.

Blessed are the merciful, for they will receive mercy.

Blessed are the pure in heart, for they will see God.

Blessed are the peacemakers, for they will be called children of God.

Blessed are those who are persecuted for righteousness' sake, for theirs is the kingdom of heaven.

Blessed are you when people revile you and persecute you and utter all kinds of evil against you falsely on my account. Rejoice and be glad, for your reward is great in heaven, for in the same way they persecuted the prophets who were before you. (Mt. 5.3–12)

The Beatitudes teach the upside-down-ness of the cruciform life. The cross exposes us to what it means to be truly human: to be vulnerable. It shows us that we are not our own. It shows us that we are, like our Lord, with others and for others. It points to the glory of the incarnate God who did for us what we cannot do for ourselves.

And in our own little corner, this is what our Lenten disciplines can do for us. They strip us bare so that we may be clothed with Christ. They are to empty us so that we may be filled by his love. They are to weaken us so that we may bear in strength the Word of reconciliation and peace. Our fears that make us draw back from this self-emptying can be calmed only by Christ's love.

Christ's Presence Even in Our Fear

But now thus says the LORD,
he who created you, O Jacob,
he who formed you, O Israel,
Do not fear, for I have redeemed you;
I have called you by name, you are mine.
When you pass through the waters, I will be with you;
and through the rivers, they shall not overwhelm you;
when you walk through fire you shall not be burned,
and the flame shall not consume you. (Isa. 43.1–2)

All three communities, the Jieng Christians, the Christians of St George's and the Melanesian Brotherhood, find God's transforming presence even in the midst of fear. At St George's, God's presence is announced at the opening of every service: *Allah hu ma'na wa Ruh al-Qudus ma'na aithan* ('God is here, and His Holy Spirit is here'). Worshippers understand what it means to be in God's presence even while in the midst of very grave danger. Fear is cast out because God is present.

And yet at St George's they have every practical reason to fear. Canon White recounts how he baptized thirteen adults in secret, all of them converts from Islam. He warned them of what they already knew: in their political context to confess Christ would open them to the dangers of abduction, rape, torture, murder. Nevertheless, these new believers insisted: they wanted to be baptized. They wanted to follow Jesus. Thirteen were baptized. Eleven of them were dead within the week. This kind of episode has repeated itself throughout the years at St George's. God's presence is desired, is assured, is even discerned, but is not mistaken for a talisman of security.

The harsh questions posed by fear also present themselves to Marc Nikkel. He asked himself why he stayed in such a life-threatening situation in Sudan. Why did his witnessing the slaughter, which left two million corpses in its wake, not propel him to abandon his mission work there? Indeed, why did his experience of being kidnapped and forced to flee on a death march not destroy his faith and spiritual strength? He asked himself concretely why he should not return to the

United States, where he could earn at least four times the salary even as a manual labourer, and where he could have built a stable life.

His own response to these questions is breathtaking. He says that he found a palpable sense of God's presence there among his people in the Sudan, a sense that he had found nowhere else. Nikkel says that he had never been so aware of God's compassion, healing and sustaining presence. He quotes Henri Nouwen's sparkling definition of compassion in *A Reflection on the Christian Life*:

> Here we see what compassion means. It is not a bending toward the underprivileged from a privileged position; it is not a reaching out from on high to those who are less fortunate below; it is not a gesture of sympathy or pity for those who fail to make it in the upward pull. On the contrary, compassion means going directly to those people and places where suffering is most acute and building a home there.[27]

God's compassion for all human life was what kept Nikkel in Sudan. More than in his home in the United States, he felt God's presence there. He was strengthened by God's loving and intimate care in his own serving, sharing and suffering with those among whom he witnessed, and who witnessed to him. The fact that God was present even when he felt entirely abandoned is the mystery that kept him from leaving.

Canon White and his parishioners at St George's also
struggled with the question of why and how to stay. One of
the stories in Scripture that empowered them in responding to
this question is the story of Elijah in the cave. God asks Elijah
that very question: 'What are you doing here, Elijah?' As we
remember, Elijah's answer is built on self-pity: he is hiding from
persecution. Canon White does not hear God commanding
him to leave his place of persecution, but to stay. He is given the
assurance of God's steadfast presence and he builds his hope on
that:

> The steadfast love of the LORD never ceases,
>
> his mercies never come to an end;
>
> they are new every morning;
>
> great is your faithfulness.
>
> 'The LORD is my portion,' says my soul,
>
> 'therefore I will hope in him.' (Lam. 3.22–24)

Even in their persecution and fear, God is found to be present,
faithful and merciful.

Brother Richard Carter of the Melanesian Brotherhood also
confesses fear, but it is not a fear of staying. It is a fear more akin
to doubt. Like Canon White and Marc Nikkel, Brother Richard
speaks of fear as seeming to interfere with his own faith. But
it is not like fear of the darkness. It is the fear of abandonment. It
is the fear even of the feeling of being abandoned by God, and

the fear that he himself is abandoning his own faith. With that fear comes the sense that God's presence is eclipsed. But even there, in the upside-down logic of the cross, he finds God to be present.

> Often I will leave this chapel feeling I have just missed what I came for, or the futility of my faith is mocking me, and yet I will long to come again and be, be more deeply. It is all we have to defeat the darkness ... I feel your presence in the night.[28]

As their Chaplain, Brother Richard feels responsible for the Brothers' safety. When some of them are taken hostage, tortured and eventually martyred, he feels not only terrible grief, but also crushing guilt. Even if God did not answer their prayers to keep the Brothers safe, why did God not at least awaken Richard to the grave danger they were facing? He questions his own judgement and discernment. But the Mission Conference facilitator to whom he pours out his lament asks him this simple question: 'Have you ever thought that God did not warn you because he wants them there?' Richard holds to this hope, even while he questions how God could knowingly subject His children to such horror. Here is living at the foot of the cross.

How can God really be present in this suffering, this torture, this murder? Brother Richard reminds himself and us that God is present wherever two or more gather in Jesus' name.

There is a Presence here that is not of this world, a Presence that pervades and invades us, a Presence that breaks through our smallness and our sinfulness, makes us better than we are, a Presence that is awfully real because it is a Person, a living, risen Person. Again and again we see in his life that Christ is the liberator, the one whose presence sets his people free.[29]

And the result of that presence is a diminishment of longing, a greater joy. This slaking of thirst at God's presence is what Augustine meant when he said 'You have made me for Yourself, and my heart will not rest until it rests in You' (*Confessions* 1.1).

For us who seek to discern what our own martyrdom might mean, even if 'only' white martyrdom, we too can be assured of God's presence. In our own loss and pain and suffering, indeed even there we can find ourselves in the very place where we are called to give testimony. We may never be Job, or Canon White, or in Melanesia, or at Bishop Gwynne College. But how will we in our otherwise humdrum lives face what may appear to be random sufferings (loss of loved ones, illnesses, impoverishments of all kinds, etc.) such that the body of Christ is built up? How can our own defence of the hope that is in us lift high the cross and glorify God? For each of us this will be different. But this is the Christian life. Our manner of living into the seemingly ordinary and random afflictions of our lives can offer them up to the 'completing of what is lacking in Christ's afflictions for the sake of his body, that is, the church' (Col. 1.24). Especially there, where the cross meets our pain, God will be present.

Questions for further reflection

- 'For just as the sufferings of Christ are abundant for us, so also our consolation is abundant through Christ' (2 Cor. 1.5). Do our own afflictions point us and others to Christ? If so, how?
- Martyrs hold before us defiantly the same question that Job answered with dogged faithfulness, the same question each of us must face every day: can we love God for God's sake alone? How do we respond to this question?
- What would it take for us to be white martyrs in our own homes, families, work lives? How do we discern God's will for us here?

8

Morning:
New Creation

*Weeping may endure for a night
But joy cometh in the morning.*

PS. 30.5, KJV

The claim that Jesus rose from the dead is key to all Christian confession. And yet, in many respects, it is one of the most difficult pieces of the Gospel story. What does it mean to claim that Jesus' dead body has emerged alive from the tomb? There is a reason we do not have any descriptions of Jesus' actual resurrection in the Gospels. Here, we have come upon an important theological fact: as we noted earlier the scene is so beyond human experience that it is not even describable. Twentieth-century New Testament scholar Rudolph Bultmann told us that modern folk have a distinctly different problem with

Jesus' resurrection and miracles than did the ancients. Modern technology, said Bultmann, has given us a fundamentally different view of 'reality' and life in the body than the ancients held. This is true, to be sure. But it is clear from the Gospels that even Jesus' disciples had a hard time with his resurrection.

For example, we might have wanted a description of Jesus exiting the tomb. One of the non-canonical gospel contains such a story. But in the canonical gospels, we simply have witnesses who tell us of an empty tomb, witnesses who pass on news of a missing body, witnesses who say that Jesus appeared to them after he died and was buried.

But even these scenes are almost unimaginable. At first the disciples cannot recognize Jesus. It takes time for them to realize that this is the same man with whom they had lived, travelled, fished and eaten. For the Christian faith to make any sense whatsoever, the claim that Jesus rose bodily from death must be reckoned with. If the whole story is going to hang together, this thing we call Jesus' resurrection cannot have been simply a resuscitation.

It is for this reason that the details of Jesus' death and burial are so important. All four canonical gospels tell us at least something about these episodes. The Apostles' Creed says: '[Jesus] suffered under Pontius Pilate, was crucified, died and was buried.' Just in case you did not catch it: He died. He was dead. He did not just appear to be dead. He was not just sleeping, or unconscious, or in a coma. The death of a human is easy enough to imagine and to describe. But the claim that Jesus rose from the dead can be a fishbone that sticks in the throat. Even the first witnesses clearly had trouble with the idea, or they would not have been expecting to find him dead.

> They have taken the Lord out of the tomb, and we do not know where they have laid him.(Jn 20.2)
>
> Why do you seek the living among the dead? (Lk. 24.5)
>
> He is not here, for he has risen. (Mt. 28)

These drip with irony. As we found earlier in chapter 5, the questions we ask and the questions we receive as responses will reveal more about us than about the risen Christ. Indeed, the most fundamental spiritual question anyone will ever face is this: why *do* we seek the Living One among the dead? Why *do* we turn elsewhere for Divine Presence when God has said 'I Am With You'? Why *are* we drawn ineluctably to things that make for death instead of that which leads to life?

'Why do you seek the living among the dead?' This is the question asked of the Mary's and Joanna. They had come to anoint Jesus' body for a proper burial. The previous day, the day Jesus died, they had to prepare for the Sabbath. The day after the Sabbath they went to the tomb clearly expecting to find nothing but a dead body. Otherwise, they would not have been bringing the spices to prepare the body for its final rest. The furthest thing from their minds was that the tomb could be empty.

Neither were they expecting the two anonymous men dressed in 'dazzling clothes' at the empty tomb, asking why they were looking for Jesus there. The men point out that Jesus had already told his friends while he was alive that he would be crucified, but that death would not hold him. Did they not remember these things?

Jesus' body is missing. But where has he gone? He rose in the shuttered darkness of the tomb, and now the stone is rolled away. The sunlight streams in. The only shadows darkening the tomb are those of John and Peter bending to look in, only half-believing the women's report.

Nineteenth-century Swiss artist Eugène Burnand rendered the scene of John and Peter racing to the tomb on the day of resurrection. The early dawn illumines the disciples' faces, revealing their eagerness, terror, disbelief, hope. Their hair and clothes fly back behind them: they are in a mad dash. Clean-shaven John clasps his hands together as if for warmth, or maybe in prayer. His young face bears a terrified look. The older Peter holds with his right hand his cloak to his left shoulder in protection from the morning chill. His furrowed brow and wide eyes show his wonder and expectation. Each man tries to outrun the other. The most striking element is Burnand's use of light. The swirling clouds beyond the disciples catch the gold of the rising sun. The day of resurrection is a day of light, as was the first day of creation. This day, however, is New Creation.

Jesus rises from death in the darkness of the tomb to come forth bringing that New Creation. On the sixth day of the creation story in Genesis 1, we read that God considered all things 'very good'. God blessed the seventh day. But we see that all quickly becomes subject to the power of death in the following episodes in Genesis. Now, God's victory at the Empty Tomb in the New Creation has set everything free from that power. New Creation means that in the Risen One we ourselves have been freed from the tyranny of evil and death. We have been rescued from the waters of the flood; we have been plucked from the waters of the raging storm on the Sea of Galilee; we have been saved from the waters of death in our baptism through which we rise in Christ to his new life.

But this New Creation does not undo the first creation. It is not as though God made a mistake on the first try and needs to start over again. That notion seems to be the heart of the story of Noah: God is horrified at the wickedness of the creatures He has made, and determines to wipe the earth clean so He can start all over. But after that episode, God promises never again to destroy His creation. We are promised a sign of His everlasting covenant: a rainbow. This refraction of light into all its colours represents the light that assures us of God's presence.

And it is not as though at the cross God mistakenly allowed the powers of Rome to snuff out the Light to the Gentiles and the glory of God's people Israel. But God did not prevent this death. Instead, He cuts through its power. Jesus is not in the sepulchre. At the empty tomb we find the dawning of the new day when God's presence will never again be withdrawn. From now on, God's light will always shine forth and illumine the dark places where death seems to rule. We have seen this in the deaths of the red martyrs and in the lives of the white martyrs. God's presence as light is there, even there.

While our Easter life is not discontinuous with the first creation, it is indeed truly new: 'Behold, I am making all things new ...' (Rev. 21.1–7). This new-yet-oldness of Jesus' life is mirrored in his charge to his disciples the night before his death: 'I give you a new commandment, that you love one another. Just as I have loved you, so you also should love one another' (Jn 13.34).

This commandment is in one respect not very new at all. It is found in the Levitical law: 'you shall love your neighbour as yourself. I am the LORD' (Lev. 19.18). The command is followed with its justification – the reason we are to love our neighbour is that the LORD is God. In the introduction to the Parable of the Good Samaritan we find this commandment from Leviticus 19.18 paired with Deuteronomy 6.5. The lawyer, at Jesus' guiding, responds to his own question about what it takes to inherit eternal life: 'You shall love the Lord your God with all your heart, and with all your soul, and with all your strength, and with all your mind; and your neighbour as yourself' (Lk. 10.27).

Yet Jesus' commandment on the night before his betrayal and death is indeed new. The love with which he loves us is a self-giving love of a kind never before encountered: 'as I have loved you'. This love makes us, the ones he loves, a New Creation. This is the kind of love commanded of us who walk in the Easter light. We are to love our neighbour not because of who the neighbour is in herself. We are to love our neighbour because of who she is in the sight of God, and in turn because of who God is. And that God has told us: 'I Am the LORD.' The One who Is: *ho on*, the Living One, the Present One. And this One is not to be found among the dead. This One is the One Who Is, and Was, and Is to Come (Rev. 1.4).

Who Is, and Was, and Is to Come

I am the Alpha and the Omega, the first and the last, the beginning and the end . . . The one who testifies to these things says, "Surely I am coming soon." Amen. Come, Lord Jesus! (Rev. 22.13, 20)

To state what may appear obvious but what could have been different, creation opens the Bible. This we saw in the first chapter. The New Creation is promised throughout the Old Testament in Israel and the prophets, and in the New Testament in Jesus and his disciples. It reappears as a confirmation at the end of the Bible: 'See, I am making all things new' (Rev. 21.5). Creation and New Creation bracket Scripture, and this is true also in our own lives before God. 'So if anyone is in Christ, there is a new creation: everything old has passed away; see, everything has become new!' (2 Cor. 5.17). 'The One who was seated on the throne said: ". . . I am the Alpha and the Omega, the beginning and the end"' (Rev. 21.6). Jesus is the beginning and the end, embracing all time, all being, everything we know and don't know, even life and death.

While the New Creation is truly new, it does not break with the first creation. The crucified and risen life of Jesus does not sneak up on us as though out of nowhere. This life is itself promised beforehand, even in Creation. Paul's letters speak of the correspondence between Adam and Christ. The first Adam is a type, or foretaste, or image, of the new Adam, who is Christ. In the first Adam, we all find that our identity holds us alienated from God (Rom. 5.12–21). This is not our true identity, however, because in our baptism into Christ's death each of us is raised to new life in him (Rom. 6.3–11). Christ is the new Adam who breathes into our *adam*-ish muddiness the spirit of life (1 Cor. 15.45). We die in Adam, but we are made alive in Christ (1 Cor. 15.22; cf. Gen. 2.7). Jesus' body dazzles and surprises and confounds. It is clearly a body made new. But he is also clearly the same Jesus as before his death. Like New Creation to first creation, Jesus is at unity with his 'old' self, and yet he is truly new.

The end of the Gospel story is like the beginning, but is even better because all in it is healed and transformed. Christ's death on the cross is not the ignominious defeat of a failed religious leader. His sacrificial death had been planned from the very beginning. The types in Leviticus are just some of the indicators of Jesus' sacrificial atoning death. The early church understood the Gospel itself to be foretold even in the curse of the Fall. The first word of Good News, the *protoevangelium*, is announced by the creator even in the curse over the serpent in the Garden of Eden. There God promised that the offspring of Eve would not ultimately be overcome by evil but would crush it: 'I will put enmity between you [the serpent] and the woman, and between your offspring and hers; he will strike your head, and you will strike his heel' (Gen. 3.15). Jesus is that offspring who crushes the head of the serpent on behalf of us who are assailed by evil and death.

The end is not unlike the beginning, but is promised to be even more remarkable. It will be shocking, in fact. God's overwhelming victory at the empty tomb surprises even those who have known Jesus best. His identity before his crucifixion, through his death, and beyond his tomb is the same. He does not change; he is the same person as before. He is the One Who Is, not another. He is the same one who said 'Before Abraham was, I AM' (Jn 8.58).

From the tomb, Jesus does not come to his friends as a spirit, an apparition, a vision. He is their very human friend. 'And while they still disbelieved for joy, and wondered, he said to them, "Have you anything here to eat?"' (Lk. 24.41, RSV). He is not a phantasm but a human body, even one who is hungry. He is their old friend.

But still, it is hard for them to recognize him. Only when he breaks bread with them and gives them a Bible lesson do they *really* recognize Jesus (Lk 24.30-31). Can you believe it? It *is* him! He is his old self, yet he is truly new. After the resurrection Jesus is recognizably the same one they knew before his crucifixion.

We find an analogous continuity/discontinuity between Jesus' day of resurrection and the creation story in Genesis 1. The day of resurrection is the day of life and light. But it is not the first day all over again. Neither is it even like the Sabbath, the crown of all creation. Jesus was dead in the tomb on the Sabbath. The first Easter (and so also every Easter since then) is a Sunday. But because the resurrection life is New Creation, it cannot be the first day of the week all over again. Neither can it be the seventh day, for that is the Sabbath. The day of resurrection is the Eighth Day.

And there was Evening, and there was Morning: the Eighth Day

A parishioner once asked me why we Christians hold our main worship on Sunday. A door-to-door missionary from a Gentile religious tradition with Christian roots had instructed her that Saturday was the only true day for worship. Our parishioner was, naturally, confused. I tried my best to explain to her that Saturday remains the Sabbath but Sunday is the Lord's Day. It is the Feast of the Resurrection. That is why even during Lent every Sunday is a feast day. Sunday as the Lord's Day is the eighth day, I said.

Our parishioner replied: 'But there are only seven days in the week. There is no eighth day.'

'That is the point,' I replied. 'Celebrating the Lord's Day as the feast of resurrection, as the Eighth Day, points us to the promised future of the New Creation. It is not another day of the week all over again. It is not the same old thing. It is a sign of the promise of God's future healing of all creation.' I don't think I convinced her.

To say that the number eight is significant throughout the Christian tradition would be a gross understatement. We might even say that the eighth day is *the* day above all other days. This is the case both in Scripture and in our worship.

This understanding of the eighth day ultimately finds its grounding, not surprisingly, in a close reading of Genesis 1.

In the first chapter, we saw that God creates in six days. God then finishes and perfects creation by blessing and resting on the seventh day, the Sabbath. While an eighth day is not specifically named in Genesis 1 (our parishioner was right in this regard), God's continuing work is implied in the mention of God's rest itself and action of perfecting and blessing (Gen. 2.2–3).

We know from a broad reading of Scripture that God is by nature unresting, unchanging, unceasing in love and power and mercy. How then could God rest? For the earliest readers of Genesis, first the Rabbis and then Christians readers, this has been a vexing question. The blessing of the seventh day is described as the final act of creation, when God blessed what He had created. It cannot mean that the God of creation is like the god of the Deists who, having created and wound the clock, walks away letting it tick-tock all by itself.

The God of Israel does not leave aside His care and sustaining grace. This God does not step offstage, but constantly watches over Israel. He guides Israel out of Egypt, reshapes them as a potter would reshape a pot, refines them with fire as gold. God's rest on the seventh day cannot indicate fatigue or boredom with what God has already done. That is not God's *modus operandi*. After all, God has just pronounced everything 'very good'. But God's blessing on the seventh day is only the prelude to the climax of New Creation on the eighth day, the day of resurrection.

The significance of the number eight is not tacked on to the thought-world of Christianity as though by a later tradition. It presents itself throughout the Bible. The number eight is woven into the instructions for the making of the framework of the tabernacle (Exod. 26.15; 36.30). It is this tabernacle where God is present with Israel as they journey out of slavery in Egypt. Jesus is that very tabernacle (Jn 1.14). Most English translations of this verse obscure the allusion: 'The Word became flesh and lived among us ...' (NRSV). A literal but more awkward translation might render the verb as either 'tabernacled', or 'pitched his tent'. God was present in the tabernacle, fashioned along dimensions governed by the number eight. So also God is present in Jesus our 'tabernacle', God-with-us in new life on the eighth day.

The circumcision of Jesus took place in accordance with the Jewish Law on the eighth day (Lk. 2.21; cf. Gen. 17.12). That the earliest church found this detail important enough to weave into the infancy stories even in Luke, the most 'Gentile' of the Gospels, is a powerful statement.

Jesse had eight sons, the youngest of whom was the little boy David. This unassuming runt of the litter would later slay the giant Goliath, the very personification of all that threatens God's promise. This eighth and last son would become the greatest King in Israel's history. But Jesse would have passed over David entirely as he brought out his sons for Samuel's inspection (1 Sam. 16). Because the LORD's favour did not fall on any of the older seven sons, Jesse was told to send for the little boy, David, who was away watching his father's flocks. David was certainly an unlikely candidate for being anointed king. But he was the LORD's choice.

Famous depictions in medieval stained-glass windows and illuminated manuscripts hold before us vividly this mystery. The image of the Jesse Tree depicts Jesus atop the tree which springs from the 'root' in Jesse's body (cf. Isa. 11.1). But why is this great King of Israel, ancestor to the Christ, not the first son of Jesse, as would be expected? If not the first, then why was he not the seventh? Seven, the number of the Sabbath day, is the number of perfection. David is beyond even perfection: he is a type of Christ. The eighth day, the day of resurrection, is beyond perfection.

The number eight plays an important role in the measurements of the new Temple in Ezekiel's vision (Ezek. 40). The cleansing of the temple lasted for eight days (1 Chr. 29.17, cf. 10). The festival of lights, Hanukkah, commemorates the eight days of the miraculous gift of oil in the lamps in the temple (1 Macc. 4.56, 59; 2 Macc. 10.6). Eight people were saved from the floods in the ark at the time of Noah (Gen. 7.7; 1 Pet. 3.20).

Because eight is a theologically significant number in the Scriptures, we find it also holds deep meaning in the Christian tradition. Within our liturgical practices, the number eight points to the hope of the resurrection. This is true of the construction of baptisteries, both buildings and fonts. Traditionally they are eight-sided. Marc Nikkel describes the chapel at Bishop Gwynne College in the Sudan as being constructed on this eight-sided plan. Even its floor tiles are octagonal. In the Middle Ages, bees were valued for their spiritual as well as economic value: their wax combs were constructed of eight-sided cells. Beeswax candles have been important liturgically throughout the centuries in part for this reason.

At the entrance to the nave in the little village church of Muros on the historic pilgrimage route of St James stands a baptismal font. As is traditional, it is eight-sided. However, there is an added feature, a very rare detail in Christian baptismal fonts. Inside the basin, carved in relief, a coiled snake lies semi-submerged in the holy water. This snake of course represents the serpent in the Garden of Eden who successfully tempted our first parents to disobedience, the disobedience which resulted in their expulsion from the presence of God. In this font's vivid imagery, the waters of baptism drown the personification of Evil. Marking our foreheads with this font's holy water in the sign of the cross recalls concretely the message of Romans 6: baptism is dying to sin with Christ and being raised with him to new life. Baptism is thus a means of return to the Garden and to the presence of God, the Tree of Life, the cross of Christ.

The light of the eighth day shines also through the floor plan of the church building. The altar traditionally faces east where the sun rises, and where morning light of the eighth day floods. The East is the source of light, and life and wisdom. In Matthew 2, the magi come from the East to pay homage to the Christ. They leave the place of light and wisdom to come to the One who is Light's source, who is Wisdom in the flesh, the One who makes even the wisdom of the world seem foolish (1 Cor. 3.19). On this journey the magi relinquish their own wisdom. They serve as types of each one of us as we too seek the Wisdom of God and the power of God in the vulnerable baby of Bethlehem.

The central part of the church in which worshipers sit (or, in some traditions, stand) is also governed by the logic of the eighth day. We call this area the 'Nave', a word derived from the Latin word for 'ship' or 'boat'. Why? The Nave is Noah's Ark, in which a remnant of humanity was saved from the waters of death. Just as Noah's family was saved from the flood, so we are saved to worship in our own Ark, the Nave (1 Peter 3:20).

Noah obeyed the command to gather into the Ark with him and his family all sorts of living creatures and even all foulness that animals bring with them. And so we too, in our Nave the Church, contend with the dung of our own inner beasts. Worshippers of the risen Lord do not claim to be free from the stains and bitterness of daily life. The Church is finally not a refuge from earthly existence, but plunges us further into it, all the while pointing to the heavenly reality. Even as we are 'surrounded by so great cloud of witnesses' in the Nave, we are still Noah's family gathered by God's mercy for safety in the Church (Heb. 12.1). But this safety includes the filth of beasts: ourselves and each other.

It is in this Church and among this Great Cloud of Witnesses that we meet Jesus. The Great Cloud is composed of remarkable and ordinary individuals throughout time: Joanna and the Marys, Peter and John, the Melanesian Brotherhood, the members of St George's, Baghdad, the missionaries in the Sudan, you and me. Without them in their time and without us in ours, Jesus would not be preached, known, worshipped and adored. We would not know him in his earthly life or in his resurrected body. Without those who wrote down the story and passed it on to us, we would not know that God is with us in light, illumining every dark corner.

> I am the light of the world. Whoever follows me will never walk in darkness but will have the light of life. (Jn 8.12)

The holy city of God will need no sun to embody the Light of Christ. There will be no more night, for God Himself will be our light (Rev. 22.5). In God's light we will see light (Ps. 36.9).

Only because we dwarves sit on the shoulders of these giants in the Great Cloud of Witnesses can we discern the light on the horizon, the morning of the eighth day. With them we are grafted as shoots into the rootstock of the people of Israel. With them we are the Body of Christ. It is in their testimony that we learn that darkness and fear are cast aside. Not without them do we find God's healing presence. It is indeed in and as the Body of Christ that we hear God's promise of His presence. 'Do not fear, for I am with you' (Isa. 41.10; 43.5). God's presence alone will satisfy our souls: 'I shall see your face; when I awake, I shall be satisfied, beholding your likeness' (Ps. 17.16).

The eighth day then is the consummation of God's grace and mercy poured out as light for the life of the world. The Eucharistic acclamation of the mystery of our faith embraces the past ('Christ has died') and the present ('Christ is risen') and the future ('Christ will come again'). The resurrection on the eighth day is a foretaste and promise of the New Creation.

But like God's rest on the seventh day of creation, Jesus' perfecting rest in the tomb is not mere sleep. On the seventh day, Jesus descends to the darkest places of humanity and brings light. He harrows Hell and sets free the prisoners bound there in death. We sometimes think of Christ's descent into Hell and releasing its captives to be 'unbiblical'. Yet we find Scriptural warrants: in Ephesians 4:9; Acts 2:24; 1 Peter 3:19; Zechariah 9:11; Ecclesiasticus 24:45 and Colossians 2:15. Likewise, Jesus' rest in the tomb on the seventh day blesses, finishes and perfects, just as did the Creator's rest on the seventh day. Jesus casts off his own grave clothes and ours, rising on the eighth day. The eighth day promises Jesus' return and initiates his continuing presence in the life of the Church.

The Gospel according to John tells us that Peter and John found in the tomb nothing except for the strips of linen used to wrap Jesus' body, along with the cloth that had covered Jesus' head rolled up neatly to the side (Jn. 20.7). Canon White of St George's tells of a middle-Eastern convention of table manners. If one needs to leave the table without having finished a meal, one neatly folds the napkin to the side. This indicates to the host that the person will return to finish the meal. Canon White interprets the detail in the Gospel according to John where Jesus' head cloth is neatly set to the side to point to Christ's promised return to the table, to be present with us in the breaking of the bread. The promise of his return is the mark of the Eighth Day. This is the promise we recite in the words of the Nicene Creed: 'He will come again in glory to judge the living and the dead, and his kingdom will have no end.' Jesus is not finished with us yet. This promise is what leans the Christian life always into the future, a future marked by eight sides, and flooded by the light of God's presence.

They shall awake as Jacob did, and say as Jacob said, Surely the Lord is in this place, and this is no other but the house of God, and the gate of heaven, And into that gate they shall enter, and in that house they shall dwell, where there shall be no Cloud nor Sun, no darknesse nor dazling, but one equall light, no noyse nor silence, but one equall musick, no fears nor hopes, but one

equal possession, no foes nor friends, but an equall communion
and Identity, no ends nor beginnings; but one equall eternity.
Keepe us Lord so awake in the duties of our Callings, that we
may thus sleepe in thy Peace, and wake in thy glory, and change
that infallibility which thou affordest us here, to an Actuall and
undeterminable possession of that Kingdome which thy Sonne our
Saviour Christ Jesus hath purchased for us, with the inestimable
price of his incorruptible Blood. Amen.

John Donne, 1627

Questions for further reflection

- Read Ephesians 5.8, 13–14: 'For once you were darkness, but now in the Lord you are light. Live as children of light … everything exposed by the light becomes visible, for everything that becomes visible is light. Therefore it says, "Sleeper, awake! Rise from the dead, and Christ will shine on you."' What blessings and commands are we given as children of the light? Does this change how we understand our place in the world?

- Why does it matter that New Creation does not 'undo' the first creation?

- Read Luke 24.36–42 and John 20.24–29. What do you think about the classic Christian claim to Jesus' bodily resurrection?

FINAL BLESSING

It seems to me that this kind of a book needs no conclusion. You, my reader, are called in your own life to live into the conclusion: the reality of God's presence. So I leave you with a simple prayer, followed by the traditional blessing from Numbers 6 with which Aaron blessed the people of Israel.

> May the Risen Lord meet you in all the places of your life, in light and in darkness, in plenty and in want, in bliss and in grief. May Eastertide be your joy, the Eighth Day your hope, and the New Creation your dwelling. Amen.

> May The LORD bless you and keep you;
> May the LORD make his face to shine upon you, and be gracious to you;
> May the LORD lift up his countenance upon you, and give you peace. (Num. 6.24–26)

ACKNOWLEDGEMENTS

Above all, I thank Archbishop Justin for inviting me to write this book for the Anglican Communion for Lent 2016. To say that I am honoured is a gross understatement. It has been my great privilege and joy. Working on this has given me a fresh encounter with the Risen Christ.

Any insights I may have offered in my close readings of Scripture owe much to the work of others, especially Karl Barth, David Weiss Halivni, Mark Kinzer, Joseph Mangina, Nahum Sarna, Christopher Seitz, Kendall Soulen and Frances Young. I continue to be grateful for the learning and witness of my professor, mentor and friend, Brevard Childs. May his memory be a blessing. It struck me well into this project how much I automatically turn first to the Old Testament to seek Jesus Christ. This is a legacy I inherit and treasure from Brevard Childs and from his own teacher, Karl Barth. However, please don't credit my faults to any of the above.

I am indebted to those who, through published writings or personal correspondence, have been a support and inspiration to me in this project: Dr Jonathan Bonk, the Revd Richard Carter, Dr Ellen Davis, Lenore Hammers, Dr Nelson Jennings, the Rt

Revd Dr Grant LeMarquand and the Revd Dr Marc Nikkel, the Revd Canon Phil Groves, Morad Mokhtari, the Revd Francis Omondi, the Revd Precious Omuku, Michele Sigg, the Revd Dr Michael Tessman, the Revd Canon Dr Jo Bailey Wells, the Revd Canon Andrew White, and my editors at Bloomsbury, Robin Baird-Smith and Jamie Birkett.

I am especially grateful to my 'support squad', Barbara Dinesen and Christina Yaworowski, and above all to my family, Matthew McCreight and our children, Noah and Grace.

ENDNOTES

1 A few technical notes:

Translation

    I will be using the New Revised Standard Version (NRSV) for Bible quotations, except where otherwise indicated. When I quote from the Psalms, I will use the translation in the Book of Common Prayer (The Episcopal Church, 1979), except where indicated.

On gendered language

    I do not fit the mould of most feminist readers of Scripture. If you are looking for the kind of inclusive language expected in many First World seminaries and 'mainline' churches, you may be disappointed. I ask simply for your charity as you read.

    While I do try my best to limit gendered language for people (other than specifically gendered characters in biblical narratives), I opt for traditional language for God. Even there, I try to limit the use of masculine pronouns for God. However, where I quote from the NRSV and the BCP, I quote directly without altering. I use more traditional and therefore gendered language especially in cases where eliminating all gendered language would either distort the translation or render it awkward.

    This means that I do occasionally refer to God with masculine pronouns. When you read the word 'He' with a capital 'H', the reference is to God. This is not to suggest that God is male, but simply to distinguish God from humanity. When you read the word 'he' with a lower-case 'h', this points to a male character, either biblical or modern. I use the word 'Lord' to refer to Jesus and the word LORD as a reference to the divine name of God.

    My use of the word LORD for the Divine Name in all capitals follows the family tradition from the King James Version through to the Revised Standard Version embraced still in the New Revised Standard Version. The word LORD is a mask for the unpronounceable but proper name of God revealed to Moses in Exodus 3.15, sometimes transliterated YHWH. This Name is sometimes referred to as the Tetragrammaton (or 'four letters'). See note 7.

If you would like further clarification on my own views on the use of 'inclusive language', the following may be of interest: *Feminist Reconstructions of Christian Doctrine: Narrative Analysis and Appraisal*. New York: Oxford University Press, 2000; 'Feminist Theology and a Generous Orthodoxy', *Scottish Journal of Theology* 57:1 (2004), 95–108; 'When I Say God, I Mean Father, Son and Holy Spirit': On the Ecumenical Baptismal Formula', *Pro Ecclesia* 6 (1997), 289–308.

Old Testament/Hebrew Bible

I have chosen not to refer to the Christian Old Testament as the 'Hebrew Bible'. Technically, the Hebrew Bible is the TANAKH, an acronym for Torah (Law), Nebi'im (Prophets) and Ketubim (Writings). This is how devout Jews refer to the Hebrew Bible. The TANAKH has its own context in the worship and prayers of the Synagogue. I retain the term the Old Testament for our context in the worship and prayers of the Church.

In part because of Martin Luther's translation of 1534, Protestants read a text that comes down to the present day through the King James Bible of 1611, which itself followed the canon of the Masoretes. This is the Second Great Rabbinic Bible (1525), also known as the Bomberg Bible, after its publisher. The Roman Catholic tradition follows the Vulgate, a 5th century translation from the Septuagint and the Hebrew texts that were available at the time to its translator, St Jerome. The Septuagint was a pre-Christian Jewish translation of the Hebrew canon of its day into Greek for Jews of the Diaspora, who lived in a mostly Greek-speaking world. Modern Christian Bibles reflect this lack of unity in the canon of the Old Testament: Protestants follow the Masoretic text while Roman Catholics and Eastern Orthodox follow the canon of the Septuagint. This is just one of the differences between Protestant and Roman Catholic/Eastern Orthodox traditions of reading Scripture. It is also just one of the elements in their respective differences in understandings of ecclesiastical authority. See note 7.

This is a very complex matter, far too deep for me to go into satisfactorily here, even if I knew enough about it to say more.

For anyone who is interested, please see the work of Kendall Soulen, Mark Kinzer and Christopher Seitz.

Gen 1.27 and the 'Image of God'

The New Revised English Version of the Bible (NRSV), which I am using in this book, mistranslates the Hebrew of Genesis 1.27. The NRSV has many strengths and weaknesses, and one of these strengths – its attempt to limit gendered language both for God and for humans – is also one of its weaknesses. I must quickly add, though, that this is not the fault of the NRSV alone. It is of the nature of translation to be inadequate no matter how astute the translator. After all, the word 'translation' in English is etymologically related to its verbal root 'to betray'.

In a well-intended attempt to rework gendered language at 1.27, the NRSV unfortunately makes the text impossible to read closely in English. At Genesis 1.26, the NRSV translation of the Hebrew word *adam* by the English word 'humanity' obscures the key concept of being created in the image and likeness of God: relation. It misconstrues not only God's relation to creation, but also the nature of the relation of humans one to another, and indeed also their relation to the rest of the created order. I will therefore try to offer my own translation and comments where necessary. Unfortunately, this will mean reintroducing some of the gendered language the NRSV has attempted to cover up, but I will try to do so as infrequently as possible. Because of this translation problem, I will try to use the transliteration of the Hebrew word rendered in the NRSV as 'humanity': *adam*.

2   John D. Zizioulas, *Being as Communion: Studies in Personhood and the Church*. London: DLT, 1985, p. 105.

3   I use the terms 'type' and 'antitype' to point to a traditional way of reading Scripture known as 'typological interpretation'. Typological interpretation traces patterns within or between characters or episodes of the Bible. The word 'type' refers to the first piece in the pattern, while the word 'antitype' refers to the final piece. For example, traditionally, Adam is taken as type of Christ, and Christ is Adam's antitype. Because this appears at least as early as Chapter 5 of Paul's Letter to the Romans (assumed to be written some 20 years after

Jesus' death), we know that this is a very early practice of Christian interpretation. Later in the history of the Christian tradition, Eve, 'The Mother of All Living', is read as a type of Mary, The Mother of All Who Live in Christ. Mary is Eve's antitype, participating as she does in the undoing of the Fall in her role as Jesus' mother. Mary in her turn is understood to be a type of the Church.

Prominent up until roughly the eighteenth century, after which it was for the most part eclipsed by historical–critical methods of reading Scripture, the practice of reading typologically has recently in some quarters experienced a small but enthusiastic revival. In one sense, typological interpretation is a way of understanding the text to speak prophetically.

There is a general misunderstanding that typological interpretation is solely a Christian attempt to link the two testaments. While it is true that patterns are often traced from Old Testament to New Testament, there is significant patterning within the Old Testament itself (eg, the expulsion from Eden to the Exile in Babylon; Joseph's sons' release from Egypt to the Exodus of Israel from Egypt; the Tabernacle to the Temple; etc). Types and antitypes are found also from New Testament to the Church. Just one example of this is Mary, as we saw above. While typological interpretation is often taken to be related to allegorical interpretation, there is no longer any firm consensus on the nature of that relationship.

4   Ibid.

5   Ibid,

6   Ibid.

7   In biblical Hebrew, vowels appear as 'points' resembling dots and dashes below the consonants. These were added in the early Middle Ages by Hebrew scribes known as Masoretes. Vowel pointing determines grammatical inflection, offering clarification on meaning, and guiding pronunciation for public reading in worship and study. However, in the TANAKH, the Divine Name is 'unpointed'. The fact that the Divine Name has no vowels protects it from defamation: it is not to be pronounced.

To say that the literature on the Divine Name is vast would be an understatement. The Divine Name is of deep theological significance not only for Jews, but also for Christians, in part for our own scriptural interpretation, but also for our relation to the people of Israel and our understanding of Jesus.

I will venture, however, to say that the entrenched (Gentile) habit of substituting for the Divine Name the terms 'Jehovah' and 'Yahweh' is at best misleading. Both terms are attempts at a spelling reconstruction of the Divine Name in Exodus 3.15. Use of the term 'Yahweh' comes into use mostly through the well-intended efforts of modern biblical scholars and translators. These words are used as substitutes for the Tetragrammaton, YHWH, or in English, LORD. But YHWH itself is an English language place-holder for the unpronounceable Name. Why then would we add vowels to make pronounceable what it is specifically not? In the tradition of English translation going back to the King James Version, the Divine Name is usually written 'LORD', all capitals. This makes it pronounceable, but only masked as according to the practice of the Synagogue.

The Jewish scribal practice of protecting and respecting the Divine Name by omitting the vowel pointing seems to have begun within the development of the Old Testament canon itself. The pronounceable 'mask' of the Divine Name is 'Adonai' (Hebrew for 'Lord'). It is used when the text is read aloud. Devout Jews sometimes use the Hebrew term 'HaShem' (literally 'The Name' in Hebrew) in conversation about the LORD. The word 'God' itself when written in English by devout Jews sometimes appears without the vowel, 'G–d', in order to continue this process of protecting the Name. In some Hebrew translations into English, the Divine Name is rendered as 'the Eternal'.

If we think we are somehow being less offensive to Jewish sensibilities regarding the Divine Name when we use either 'Yahweh' or 'Jehovah', we are surely mistaken. Christian confession itself is in most respects nothing other than an offence to Jewish devotion and piety. Trying to paper over this by reconstructing the Hebrew Divine Name is not going to help matters. What will help, it seems to me, is how we educate our own community to respect Jewish practice and worship. Thus we might respect the Jewish people to be themselves in their own right rather than a piece of us and thereby replaced by the Church. While Christians rightly understand ourselves to have been grafted into the root of Jesse (cf. esp. Rom. 9–11), we must not girdle the root or treat it as though it were dead.

While the Divine Name is unpronounceable, the God it names is not empty of identity. As we will find in Exodus 3.14–15, the four consonants (YHWH) are related to the verb 'to be'. In 3.14 God hints at what the Name signifies before actually revealing it: '"I AM WHO I AM…" Thus you shall say to the Israelites "I AM has sent me to you"' (Exod. 3.14). God explains that He is Being, Creating, Sustaining in freedom.

The Name of this sovereign One is presented to Moses within a personally and historically narrated context: this YHWH is the God of the promise ('the God of Abraham, Isaac and Jacob …' [Exod. 3.16]) and the One who will liberate the people from slavery so that they can worship the LORD (3.17, cf. 12).The Name attends a relationship and does not introduce a vague or generic 'unknowable' deity.

8   This is one of many places where we see how Old Testament functions within itself as prophecy and fulfilment. Prophecy and fulfilment motifs are not simply a Christian innovation, as though externally imposed to link the New Testament to the Old Testament, or to 'prove' the truth of the Gospel. Types and their antitypes function also internally to each Testament.

9   Notice that there is one calf Aaron makes, but he introduces it as though it were more than one: your gods. This harks back to the earlier name for God, Elohim, which evokes a plural form even though used as a singular noun. It is as though at the episode of the Golden Calf Israel has turned back the clock as if they had never learned God's proper name or identity.

10   On 'type', see note 3.

11   Christian Wiman, *My Bright Abyss*. New York: Farrar Straus Giroux, 2013, p. 22.

12   Here is just one of the reasons why I believe that it is misguided to call the Christian Old Testament the Hebrew Bible.
     Malachi is the final book of the Old Testament, but it is not the final book of the Hebrew Bible. In fact, the Hebrew Bible ends

with 2 Chronicles. In the Hebrew Bible, Malachi comes between Zechariah and the Psalms. Thinking about why this is so has filled volumes.

It is at the very least important for Christians to be aware that the Synagogue does not read the Hebrew Bible in the same way as we read our Old Testament. Nor does the Hebrew Bible have a similar communal and theological role in the Synagogue that our Old Testament has for us. This is only in small measure because of the ordering of the canon.

The Synagogue reads differently for very good reasons. These reasons include the firm 'no' that the Synagogue gives to the Church's claims about Jesus and his relationship to Israel's God and Scriptures. The Church must respect this 'no' without sidelining, as though in embarrassment, our own 'yes'. Calling our Old Testament the Hebrew Bible in hopes of making these matters seem more 'objective' or 'scholarly' and therefore less chafing religiously only obscures the issues as in euphemism. While washing ourselves of the stains of our antisemitisms past and present is crucial, this is not the effective or proper place to do so. It distorts our own tradition and risks being condescending to the Jewish people.

13   In the King James Version, this phrase was translated as 'a still small voice'. This is often taken to mean that Elijah enters some sort of spiritual state. The application is then made that we also are to calm and quiet our minds in stillness and meditation in order to invite the voice of God to come into our hearts. Preachers of the late twentieth century devoured this interpretation. However, the storyline of 1 Kings 19 makes it clear that Elijah enjoys no pleasurable, calming, meditative experience. Instead, he encounters God as alien presence.

14   The story of the rabbi in the concentration camp is, I believe, either from David Weiss Halivni or Peter Ochs. I cannot find the reference now. I believe that the term I am using to describe God as 'alien presence' is also Halivni's.

15   This formula is similar to the one at the opening of Nathan's parable in 2 Samuel 12.1. See also Esther 2.5. Nathan's parable in 2 Samuel is not set in time and space. It is simply an illustration narrated within

the larger realistic narrative of King David's sin against Bathsheba and her husband, Uriah. The parable is told for the purpose of opening David's eyes to his own sin. Like the man in Nathan's parable, Job is not to be read as a historical character. He is an illustration. This will make Job's function as witness to Christ that much more effective. We will see how in this supra-historic element, Job is very different from Jesus, even while a witness to him.

16 While Hebrews 5–7 makes much of Melchizedek, that character does not play much of a role in Scripture. See also Genesis 14.18 and Psalm 110.4. Job plays only a slightly greater role in the rest of the canon than does Melchizedek.

17 The word translated here 'to curse' is in Hebrew literally the verb 'to bless'. It is the context that determines the meaning. One gets the impression that cursing God is beyond the realm of possibility: 'How could the word "curse" ever appear in relation to God? Its opposite must be used instead.' Why should Job even care about cursing God or not, since he is not of Israel? Yet this respect for God is on his lips as well. Even as an alien, Job is nevertheless faithful.

18 See note 3.

19 Ibid.

20 Frances Young, *God's Presence: A Contemporary Recapitulation of Early Christianity*. Cambridge: Cambridge University Press, 2013, p. 58.

21 Simone Weil, *Gateway to God*. Fontana, 1978, pp. 48, 55.

22 The Melanesian Brothers are an Anglican Community based mainly in the Solomon Islands.

23 Andrew White, *Faith Under Fire: What the Middle East Conflict Has Taught Me About God*. Oxford/Grand Rapids: Monarch, 2011.

24 Marc Nikkel and Grant LeMarquand (ed.), *Why Haven't You Left? Letters from the Sudan*. New York: Church, 2006.

25 Richard Anthony Carter, *In Search of the Lost: The Death and Life of Seven Peacemakers of the Melanesian Brotherhood*. Norwich: Canterbury Press, 2006.

26   White, *Faith Under Fire*, p. 132.

27   Nikkel and LeMarquand, *Why Haven't You Left?*, p. 134.

28   Carter, *In Search of the Lost*, p. 135.

29   Ibid., p. 196.